Running in Place

Running in Place

A Campaign Journal

Bruce E. Altschuler

State University of New York at Oswego

Nelson-Hall Publishers / Chicago

Library of Congress Cataloging-in-Publication Data

Altschuler, Bruce E.
    Running in place : a campaign journal / Bruce E. Altschuler.
        p.   cm.
    ISBN 0-8304-1439-8
    1. Elections—New York (State)—Case studies. 2. Electioneering—
—New York (State)—Case studies. I. Title.
JK3492.A48   1996
324.9747'043—dc20   95-21336
                                                                                  CIP

Photo credits: July 4th photo by Bruce Altschuler. All other photos courtesy of Bill and Louise Scheuerman.

Typesetter: Fine Print, Ltd.
Printer: Capital City Press

Manufactured in the United States of America

10 9 8 7 6 5 4 3 2 1

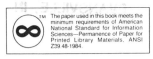

The paper used in this book meets the minimum requirements of American National Standard for Information Sciences—Permanence of Paper for Printed Library Materials. ANSI Z39.48-1984.

Contents

Acknowledgments

A few words cannot begin to express the debt I owe to Bill and Louise Scheuerman. Not only was Bill responsible for getting me a teaching job at SUNY Oswego, his and Louise's friendship sustained me through some very difficult years after that. To me, they are family. I can only hope that my writing skills are sufficient to show what admirable people they are. I ask their indulgence for any parts of the book that did not come out right.

I would also like to thank my brother Glenn for his helpful ideas about turning the original journal into a book. Thanks to Richard Meade and Rachel Schick of Nelson-Hall for their suggestions for improving the structure and flow of the original manuscript.

Ordinarily, this is when the author, having thanked others for their help, accepts the blame for any errors that remain. Because the focus of this book is a campaign, such errors are different in kind from other books. The journal represents my feelings and perceptions at a particular time. It therefore reflects incomplete, sometimes inaccurate, information set down in the heat of the moment. Often, later entries correct such misperceptions, but if any have resulted in inaccurate portrayals of people involved, I hope they understand. I have tried to give a more objective analysis in the concluding chapter but believe that the journal is particularly worthwhile because it conveys the sense of what it is like to be involved in politics—the hopes and frustrations, the excitement and disappointment. Any attempt to make it more objective and fair would tamper with that. Most of the people portrayed in the journal worked hard out of idealistic motives. I hope that I have conveyed that to a wider public that is often cynical about politics.

Introduction

With so many articles and books about political campaigns, why do we need another, especially one about an election in a rural county in upstate New York? The simple answer is that such campaigns are more important than we may think. Despite the voluminous literature on elections, these campaigns have been little studied. For a long time, most writing on political campaigns concentrated on presidential elections. Although more attention has been paid to other campaigns, that work has focused on congressional and statewide contests rather than the local elections that comprise the largest number of campaigns in the United States.

Thus, Doris Graber writes that research on the effects of mass media on elections is quite unbalanced:

> Presidential elections have been extensively studied, and congressional elections have drawn the attention of more and more scholars. Far less is known about the media's role in gubernatorial elections and practically nothing about their impact on local, judicial, or school board elections.[1]

Those studying other aspects of political campaigns have come to similar conclusions. According to John Frendreis and Alan Gitelson, "the study of local party organizations has, for too long, been relegated to a minor role compared to the study of national and state party organizations." Anthony Gierzynski believes, "It is no exaggeration to say that political scientists' knowledge of legislative elections is based almost entirely on research dealing with congressional elections. The nature of state legislative elections has been largely inferred from the studies at the national level."[2]

One reason for this is the large number of local elections. As Frank Sorauf writes, "Because their political institutions, history, traditions, and politics differ greatly, the 50 states are the curse of any commentary about American politics."[3] As a result, studies of local parties and campaigns have tended to focus on those easiest to study—urban districts with highly visible mass media coverage. One recent work, despite the title *Political Parties in Local Areas*, is a collection of articles about urban political parties in the cities of Houston, Nashville, Chicago, Detroit, and Los Angeles. Similarly, Samuel Eldersveld's classic theory of the political party is based on a study of Detroit. According to Sorauf, information about the costs of local campaigns comes "almost entirely from newspaper reports and primarily of big city mayoral races."[4]

The very fact that the campaigns studied are so much more visible than those that are not studied indicates at least one significant difference between them. Are there others? This book will examine a low-visibility state legislative campaign in great detail. In it, Democrat Bill Scheuerman runs for the New York State Assembly in a district that strongly favors the Republican party. Such less-publicized campaigns are the bread and butter of American politics. As one group of scholars has argued, "Vital as presidential and statehouse politics may be, it is in the localities that the voters are found and electoral politics conducted. What happens in the 3,600 county and equivalent jurisdictions determines the politics of states and the nation."[5]

In order to put the 117th Assembly District election into a larger context, we must understand the different actors in local campaigns. To do this, we will examine the scholarly literature to see what it tells us about political parties, candidates and their strategy, the role of money, interest groups, the media, and the goals of campaigns. These findings will be applied to the particular situation of Oswego County, and more particularly, Bill Scheuerman's campaign for the New York State Assembly. Following the more detailed examination of this campaign, we will seek to draw larger conclusions. Of course, a study of a single campaign, no matter how detailed, cannot provide definitive answers, but it can tell us something about the nature of today's campaigns. It can also tell us whether the lack of attention to elections of the type portrayed in this book requires a reconsideration of what we think we know about the modern political campaign.

Political Parties

Most of the recent debate about American political parties discusses whether or not they have declined.[6] As L. Sandy Maisel puts it,

"The conventional wisdom, simply stated, is that a major change has occurred in the last two decades, a change from old to new politics." In other words, party-centered personal campaigning has been largely supplanted by the candidate-centered, media-oriented campaign. However, Maisel does not fully agree with this argument, claiming instead that "new politics has replaced old politics in some areas, for some offices. Often this change is more subtle than bold." With the two types continuing to coexist, there remains considerable truth to Tip O'Neill's oft-quoted statement that "all politics is local."[7] Graber also argues that although the growth of the mass media has led to a decline in the importance of party affiliation in national elections, it "remains very important at the state and local levels where the average voter knows little about most candidates, and media information is scant, particularly on television." Another view is that parties have become less important as a cue to voters at the same time that party organizations have actually become stronger by adapting to modern campaign technology.[8]

To evaluate this argument we need to understand the role currently played by political parties. Because of our federal system, American party organizations operate at three levels that are separate but interdependent: national, state, and local. The election we will look at is too remote from the national scene for either the national Republican or Democratic parties to have paid much attention, but both state and local parties had a role to play. One of the adaptations of state party organizations has led them to provide campaign services and other resources to selected local candidates. In general, aid is targeted to those believed to be most competitive. To show the extremes to which such targeting has gone, Ruth Jones cites the Idaho Republican Party which, even after targeting specific districts, did not distribute any money until it had reviewed candidate strategy.[9] In Oswego County, party registration so strongly favors the Republicans that the Democrats have won only one assembly race in the last one hundred years. In order to win, Democrat Scheuerman needed significant outside help. Given his own and his local party's limited resources, the most logical source of help was his state party, but he could get it only if he could convince that party that he had a reasonable chance of winning. Conversely, he could have such a chance only if adequate funding was available. Finding a way out of this vicious circle was an early priority for his campaign. Further complicating his situation was the fact that the Democratic Party already had a majority

3

in the Assembly, a majority that did not appear in jeopardy during the 1990 election. On the other hand, it was the Republicans who controlled the Senate. Thus, it was more likely that the state Democratic party would pump money into questionable senate races than comparable ones for the assembly.[10]

The local party plays a more direct role in state legislative elections. Although there are city, town, and village party committees, it is generally the county party that is most important. But how important and in what ways? The major comprehensive study of local party organizations found that most are highly personalized with little or no bureaucratic structure. County chairs are primarily part-time and unsalaried, working an average of twelve hours per week during the election period and less than two-and-a-half hours per week the rest of the year. Only 10 percent of county parties have a paid staff while fewer than 15 percent have a phone listing. During the campaign season, a majority have campaign headquarters, 79 percent distribute literature, 70 percent arrange fund raisers, 65 percent give money to candidates, 62 percent organize phone campaigns, over 50 percent send mailings, and nearly 50 percent organize door-to-door canvassing, but only 33 percent buy broadcast time and less than 15 percent use polls.[11] The Oswego County Democratic Party was very much a skeletal organization, headed by an unsalaried part-time chair, Lou Iorizzo, and dependent upon the generosity of local volunteers for virtually all of its activities.

Does it matter that most local parties are not headed by full-time chairs? One group of scholars argues that although "there is some tendency for amateurs to head weaker local party organizations," the direction of causality is unclear and that it is likely "that amateurism/purism has not weakened party organizations."[12]

A major function of political parties is the recruitment of candidates. According to Eldersveld, the party both persuades good candidates to run and screens out bad candidates. He sees recruitment as a five-stage process. From the available pool of possibilities, the party: (1) identifies those it may support (Discovery); (2) tests candidate support both within and outside the party organization (Negotiation); (3) makes a formal endorsement (Sponsorship); (4) mobilizes support for its candidate (Campaign); and (5) lets the voters decide (Election). Because the ability to recruit able leaders is crucial to the party's existence, the final party choice "is the result of much testing, screening and consultation."[13] In real life such a tidy rational model rarely holds up. Nevertheless, if it is worthwhile it should describe the essence of the nominating process. In our conclusion, we will examine how well it described the process by which Bill Scheuerman was nominated by his party.

Finally there is the question of party effectiveness. To put it another way, does the strength and activity of a local party have an effect on election results? Although the answer to this may seem obvious, existing research is far from conclusive. V. O. Key claims that high levels of interparty competition are associated with strong party organizations, a claim echoed by one group of scholars who write that "the relative organizational strength of the parties in a system will find some reflection in the vote."[14]

However, a more recent evaluation of published studies by a group that includes one of the above scholars concludes that "although suggestive, the limited geographic scope or earlier time frame of this research leaves open the question of the contemporary electoral relevance of party organizations." One reason is that the objective of contesting and winning elections depends on the situation a party finds itself in. "For example, in areas of one-party dominance the minority party may follow a long-term developmental approach that includes establishing a token presence, developing a cadre of local activists, and gradually recruiting (or converting) credible candidates." Such an organization would be more interested in recruiting good candidates than mass efforts to win votes. Their own study shows little direct effect on vote totals from either party activity or organizational strength but that parties have an indirect effect on the vote by being able to offer a full slate of candidates.[15]

Gerald Pomper argues that parties have even less effect than that. His study of gubernatorial and state legislative elections in New Jersey concludes:

> Parties appear to have their primary effect on turnout at the registration stage. Beyond that, the possibility of influencing participation drops drastically.
> Effective parties, then, may best demonstrate their effectiveness before and between elections. Their campaign activities are relatively marginal.

Pomper finds that the major determinants of election results are demographic factors and party registration. Measures of party organization and activity show little relation to electoral success. In contrast to Pomper's findings, an examination of party contacts of voters in South Bend, Indiana, finds that the effects of such contacts are more indirect. Parties contacted those voters most receptive to their message in the hope that they would do more than simply vote for the party candidate. By getting these supporters to contribute money, put up yard signs and bumper stickers, and speak to their neighbors, the original contact could have a ripple effect. "Party organizations mobilize the faithful, and the activity of the faithful sends a message to the rest of the public."[16]

Most of this research, if accurate, makes the uphill struggle of candidates like Bill Scheuerman seem nearly hopeless. Later in this introduction, we will show how much of a disadvantage party registration and demographic factors placed him at. As a political scientist, Bill was surely aware of such difficulties. If even organizing his party to heightened levels of activity would not be likely to improve his chances enough to win, why run? In a study of congressional candidates, Maisel argues that the decision to run is one of the most difficult and least understood aspects of the electoral process. Although these are individual decisions made for a variety of reasons, "cumulatively they have an important impact on congressional elections in various districts and throughout the nation."[17]

Candidates and Their Strategy

Anyone who decides to run for office faces a series of immediate decisions. Marjorie Randon Hershey points to three major tasks facing a candidate at the beginning of a campaign. The first is developing an organization. This involves recruiting a campaign manager and other staff as well as a setting up a division of labor among them. For a volunteer organization such as Bill's simply finding qualified, motivated people proved to be one of the most difficult aspects of the campaign. With no salaries and the odds against electoral success, maintaining that motivation was also a formidable job. One of the surprises of the campaign was that, despite many ups and downs, the level of candidate and organizational morale remained incredibly high. In our conclusions we will try to explain why this occurred.

Hershey's second task is gathering information about the district, its major groups and leaders, and the strengths and weaknesses of the potential opposition. Third is deciding how to present the candidate. What qualifications should be stressed? How can the candidate best identify with the needs of the constituency?[18]

For Maisel, the key question in starting an organization is the strength of the local party. "Campaigns using the party organization work well," he maintains, "if there is a party organization. How does a candidate run when the party organization is nonexistent or inactive, as is the case in many counties throughout the country? Or how does a candidate run if the opposition party is stronger in his or her district, making it necessary to appeal to those in the other party?" Because Bill Scheuerman ran in a district dominated by the opposition party, Maisel's answer is of considerable interest to us. It is his view that local candidates in this situation need to resort to old-fashioned personalized campaigning, which necessitates establishing a volunteer organization whose workers should campaign only for that candidate.

Despite its apparent inefficiency, such an approach is best because it shows that this candidate is different and has people who care enough to go door-to-door on his or her behalf.[19] However, we can see potential conflict between a candidate using this approach and the political party. Considering how few resources the Oswego Democratic Party had, it was obvious that seeing candidates appropriate some of its best workers for their own purposes would cause strains between the two. The party wanted to tie all its candidates together both organizationally and in their appeals while candidates, especially in districts where their party suffered from a significant numerical disadvantage, found that the only possible winning strategy was to emphasize their independence from the party. We will see such tensions periodically flaring up in Bill Scheuerman's campaign. In our conclusions we will evaluate the pluses and minuses of such candidate-centered volunteer organizations.

Hershey's second and third tasks are made difficult because, as she puts it, "so few of the stimuli into a campaign actually come directly from the voters." The most obvious ways to discover the concerns of voters are polls and canvassing, but "public opinion is a slippery and sensitive thing," while the need to interpret the raw data of polls means that voters' views will be filtered through the beliefs and experiences of the poll-taker or analyst. Canvassing is potentially even less accurate since it is generally done by volunteers whose strong support for the candidate can easily bias their results. The costs in time and money may also put such methods out of the reach of many local candidates. Thus, candidates are likely to look to political activists such as group leaders, local elites, organized interests, or their own leading supporters,

7

creating the danger that the campaigner will concentrate more on issues that matter to political elites than to most voters.[20] This difficulty plagued Bill Scheuerman's campaign as he could never be certain where he stood with the voters at any particular time. As we shall see, positive information was far more likely to come to the candidate's attention than were signs of weakness. The lack of objective information also made it more difficult to convince the state party and interest groups that Bill's chances of winning were good enough to justify significant financial assistance. How this information dynamic affected the campaign will be a constant theme of the journal that follows.

Having organized the campaign, the candidate must now go out in search of votes. Although it hardly requires a political scientist to understand that the main goal of most candidates is to win the election, how to do so is a far more difficult question. William Crotty reflects the consensus among scholars, writing that the major methods for practical politicians "are to activate latent support and reinforce inclinations among sympathetic voters to support their party and its candidates."[21] If, however, campaigns primarily mobilize already existing support rather than convert nonsupporters or even opponents, it is likely that they will not have very much effect on election outcomes unless the race is so close that even a small shift will change the result. This is confirmed by Susan Howell and William Oiler's study of New Orleans local elections, which finds that even in a nonpartisan election, campaign activities have a limited effect on the results, explaining less than one-fifth of the variance. Gerald Kramer's examination of precinct-level canvassing shows some effect on voter turnout but very little on voter preferences for either national or local office. Nor did repeated contacts make any significant difference.[22]

It is unlikely that many candidates share this view for, if it is true, they are wasting considerable time and money. Fortunately for them, recent work suggests that the theory of minimal campaign effects has become less applicable as party identification among voters has weakened.[23] Gary Jacobson points out that about 13 percent of voters in presidential elections change their minds from one election to the next and between 7 and 10 percent during a campaign. Local elections present even greater possibilities for change because the candidates start with less well-defined identities than those at the national level. Jacobson's hypothesis is that "broadcast campaigning will have its greatest effect in elections for offices other than U.S. President." His argument is supported by

Tedin and Murray's study of Texas statewide elections, which finds even greater voter volatility with 18 percent changing their minds during the primary and 26 percent during the general election. They suggest that conversion is greater than at the presidential level because voters have less information at the start of a campaign and there is less free media coverage, allowing the candidates' advertising to make up a larger proportion of available knowledge. Their conclusion is that "electoral success thus comes to depend more than ever on the personal attributes of the candidates and their ability to raise funds and exploit modern technologies."[24]

How does this argument apply to a campaign such as the one we are looking at? The national trend of weaker party loyalty is likely to apply to the 117th Assembly District. In addition, public knowledge of candidates for state legislature, especially for an open seat, will be very limited. But what if the potential is not matched by the availability of means for taking advantage of it? As we shall see, media, primarily radio, was used by both candidates. Television, however, was not a factor. On the other hand, the population of the district was far smaller than those of the above studies. Could the combination of modest media use and traditional politics result in significant conversion? For Bill Scheuerman this would be the most crucial question of the campaign. A positive answer would at least open up the possibility of victory; a negative one would ensure defeat. In our conclusions, we will try to provide an overview of his efforts at conversion and why they did or did not succeed.

Whatever the available means, candidates must determine how best to appeal to the voters, Hershey's third task. Richard Joslyn suggests four types of appeals: partisan, personal characteristics, demographic group identities, and issues. He further divides issue appeals into three types. In the first, candidates simply emphasize how important the issue is without explaining what actions they would take if elected. Vague, ambiguous, or symbolic appeals constitute the second type. The third type consists of specific policy proposals. Joslyn's study of campaign advertising finds that "what the ads definitely do *not* contain are partisan and specific issue appeals." Instead, candidates use issues to show their personal attributes. Since 1969, Joslyn maintains, "ads have become less partisan, less filled with specific issue information, and considerably more group-oriented."[25]

Even though the election we are examining is very different from those studied by Joslyn, we will see that the pattern of appeals

9

is quite similar. Nevertheless, reducing issue content does not eliminate it entirely. As suggested in the previous paragraph, candidates' appeals use general issue themes to demonstrate why they are personally better qualified than the opposition.[26] Thus, a candidate may urge more aid to the homeless as a way of contrasting him or herself to a less caring opponent. The advocacy of capital punishment is a common tactic to show a tough approach to crime and concern for the victims of crime. Because these positions are chosen to utilize a theme important both to the candidate and a majority of the electorate, the only problem for the campaign is how best to present them. But what happens when a candidate has an opinion that a large majority of the voters does not agree with? Of course the candidate can try to concentrate on other subjects, but if the troublesome issue is important enough it may prove impossible to avoid. Reporters will persist in asking about it or it may come up during a debate.

To what extent should candidates be willing to modify their views to accommodate constituency opinion? The candidate may stand firm, hoping that the voters will admire a person of principle or that other issues will prove more important to them. However, if that is not the case, should the candidate conclude that a change of opinion on one issue is worthwhile in order to get elected and get other things accomplished? Another rationale for modifying one's position would be that democracy requires politicians to heed the views of voters. The debate over whether officeholders should consider themselves instructed delegates of the voters or use their own independent judgment goes back hundreds of years, at least to Edmund Burke. For Bill Scheuerman, it would prove to be far more than an academic exercise.

Campaign Spending

As with political parties, those who study campaign financing disagree about the extent to which the expensive new politics of the mass media campaign has replaced the more traditional party-oriented personal campaign. While the Federal Election Commission provides systematic information about spending on presidential and congressional campaigns, there is no equivalent for state and local elections. Ruth Jones argues that this lack of information is less important than it once was because "federal and state legislative campaigns are becoming more similar than they are different, and that the differences that remain are primarily of degree not kind." She supports this by showing dramatic increases in spending in Wisconsin, New Jersey, California, Florida, Washington, and Arizona. This additional money was spent on polls, consultants, direct mail, radio, and television; the major tools of the new-style campaign.[27]

Not all scholars agree. According to Susan Howell, candidates for lower office find it difficult to raise the kind of money needed for the modern-style campaign because the offices they seek have fewer powers and less visibility. Instead they are forced to rely on a more indirect approach, seeking aid from their party, other officeholders, and interest groups. Thus, such expensive campaign activities as polling and broadcast advertising are used far more for higher levels of office.[28] Sorauf agrees that changes in campaigns:

> have filtered down to local elections very unevenly. Most candidates for state legislatures do not take polls and do not have campaign consultants; moreover, they cannot efficiently use the mass media in legislative districts that are only slivers of radio and TV markets. Old-fashioned door-to-door canvassing and "literature drops," even local meetings and rallies, are much more typical of their campaigns. Moreover, their limited visibility and name recognition make it hard for them to raise money in the new ways. In short, the older modes of campaigning often result in older and more modest systems of finance.[29]

We shall see that this was very much the case in the race for the 117th Assembly District seat.

Interest Groups

Because so many Americans view interest groups as the bane of the political system, as evidenced by such common terms as special interests or pressure groups, a more neutral definition is necessary if we are to understand the role these groups play in local elections. In essence, an interest group is an organization of individuals bound together by shared attitudes and concerns who seek to influence government.[30]

In recent years, interest groups have played an increasingly active role in electoral politics. Although V. O. Key writes in 1964 that, unlike political parties, organized groups primarily "promote

11

their interests by attempting to influence government rather than by nominating candidates and seeking responsibility for the management of government," only sixteen years later, Dennis Ippolito and Thomas Walker claim that, "Interest group participation in elections is widespread . . . By participating in the selection of public officials, interest groups lay the foundation for future direct lobbying of officeholders."[31] More recently, Maisel describes interest groups as playing "a central role in the electoral process."[32]

Although it might appear that such an increased role for interest groups has come at the expense of political parties, Allan Cigler believes it is better to view their relationship as "competitive yet symbiotic." Despite competing for resources and the allegiance of officeholders, parties often court interest groups to supply campaign resources and help build coalitions.[33] In essence, interest groups are simply filling the power vacuum created by an already weakened party system. As Paul Peterson puts it, "strong parties and centralized decision making leave interest groups in a relatively disadvantageous position."[34] The current weakened party system, coupled with the decentralization of decision making in our fragmented political system, has reduced that disadvantage considerably. In addition, the smaller number of voters in local districts serves to strengthen interest groups. The diversity of groups in a national or statewide election diminishes the power of any single group.[35] In contrast, a single-issue group may represent a significant proportion, sometimes even a majority, of voters in smaller constituencies.

For Bill Scheuerman, the weakness of the local party forced him to seek help elsewhere. The most obvious source of desperately needed funds was interest groups. Like many other candidates, he actively courted those interest groups who shared his views in the hope that their endorsements would provide favorable publicity and their treasuries money. But prying that money loose was not easy. The contributions by interest groups' Political Action Committees (PACs) go largely to incumbents.[36] To get a share of the limited funds distributed to those not running for reelection, Bill had to seek out those PACs that found him significantly better than his opponent. Ninety-five percent of PACs fall into four categories: corporate, labor, trade or membership, and those not connected with a specific interest group.[37] Bill's union and education experience coupled with the fact that he was more liberal on most issues than his opponent were the parameters in deciding which groups to approach. However, he had to convince them not only that he was the better candidate but also that he had a reasonable chance of victory. Once again the vicious circle of needing money to have a chance of winning but only having a chance of winning by already having money appeared.

Media Coverage

In the modern political campaign, the mass media play an indispensable part; yet the way in which they cover election campaigns has received considerable criticism. Typical is that of Richard Joslyn who writes that "the focus on the horse race and on personal rather than political attributes of candidates would seem to make learning about the governing capabilities and policy preferences of candidates extremely unlikely." The evidence he examined indicates that neither television nor newspapers contributes much to voter understanding of the policy positions of candidates. "Strange though it may seem," he concludes, "campaign news coverage may not generally extend public understanding of public policy questions." Doris Graber's review of research on the subject also shows that the media prefers stories with dramatic conflict rather than substantive (and often complicated) issues. In her view, "It is extremely difficult for the media to mesh the public's preference for simple dramatic stories with the need to present sufficient information for issue-based election choices. Information that may be crucial for voting decisions may not appeal to much of the audience and will therefore be ignored."[38]

In the race we will examine, neither of the candidates was well known in the district at the beginning of the campaign. This was more of a problem for Bill Scheuerman than for his opponent. Bill had to give the voters good reason to change their traditional allegiances. If both candidates remained little known, he would certainly lose. Although personal campaigning provided some exposure, the size of the district meant that the only way to reach most voters was through the media. Bill's limited advertising budget forced him to rely on free media to get his message across. But the media have conflicting goals. As Robert Entman writes, "The media are expected both to be market-driven, profit-oriented organizations, which ensures they will please audiences (and therefore advertisers), and to be autonomous, free of fear or favor, which ensures they can provide truth."[39] How did the media juggle these priorities and what effect did that have on the strategies and tactics of the candidates? Did it affect the result of the election? We will see in both the campaign journal and our conclusions that these effects were of the greatest importance.

Evaluating the Campaign

Thus far, we have examined campaigns primarily from the viewpoints of the candidates and their parties. They evaluate the campaign process by judging whether it maximizes their chance of electoral success. However, we expect the public to have a very different standard of what constitutes a successful campaign. In Eldersveld's words, "how well does the campaign involve the public and contribute to meaningful citizen deliberation and decisions about political candidates, parties, and programs?"[40] The potential conflict between these goals is apparent. If the best way to win an election is the avoidance of citizen deliberation, candidates are likely to do so. Further complicating the evaluation of any election campaign is the bluntness of the choice offered to the voter who can choose a candidate but cannot add an explanation of that choice. Thus, a vote cast with extreme reservations cannot be differentiated from one cast with great enthusiasm. One voter may choose on the basis of issues; another on candidate qualifications or partisanship.

Nevertheless, we can examine the information provided by the candidates, parties, and media during the campaign. How meaningful was the discussion? Was adequate information presented to voters who wished their participation in the process to be meaningful? These are the most important questions this book will address.

The 117th Assembly District

The body of this book is my journal of Bill Scheuerman's campaign for the New York State Assembly seat representing Oswego County. The county has a population of approximately 123,000 in two cities and twenty-two towns.[41] The largest city is Oswego, whose population is nearly 20,000. The only other city in the county is Fulton, with a population of about 13,000. Thus, nearly three-fourths of the county's population live in the towns. Since the normal Democratic strategy is to aim for large majorities in the two cities to overcome the strong Republican edge in the towns, it is not surprising that only one Democrat has been elected during the past one hundred years of biennial elections. The party registration figures make the futility of this strategy clear. In the city of Oswego, there are 4,102 registered Democrats and 3,933 Republicans out of 10,371 voters. In Fulton, the Republicans have a significant registration edge of about 3,500 to 1,900 out of a total of 6,300. The Democrats' situation is far worse in the towns, where they trail with fewer than 9,000 to the opposition's nearly 24,000. Countywide, out of a total of 55,542 registered voters, 31,227 are Republicans compared to 14,876 Democrats, a greater than two-to-one edge.

The closest race during the previous decade was for the open seat in 1980 with Republican Ray Chesbro defeating Michael Yerdon by about 4,700 votes out of nearly 37,000 votes cast. Even this was a margin of 56 to 44 percent, not a particularly close contest. Furthermore, Yerdon was an unusual Democrat, a conservative from the rural northern part of the district. Thus, he was able to capture a number of the towns. On the other hand, although he carried the city of Oswego by about a thousand votes, he lost Fulton by more than eight hundred. Soon after the election, Yerdon switched to the Republican Party and, in 1990, hoped to gain that party's nomination for the Assembly seat from which Chesbro had retired.

Once Chesbro became established in office, he had little trouble from Democratic challengers. In 1982, his first race as an incumbent, he defeated Kenneth Boutwell by slightly more than two to one. The Democrats allowed him to run unopposed in 1984. In 1986, Jim McMahon's investment of $20,000 of his own money to oppose Chesbro did not prevent the incumbent from overwhelming him, with 20,075 votes to McMahon's 8,400. Not surprisingly, Chesbro was again unopposed in 1988.

In 1990, Chesbro announced his retirement. Thus, it was clear to the Democratic Party that not only was this their best chance in years to win the seat but also that, if they failed, the seat would likely belong to the newly elected Republican for as long as he or she wished to retain it.

The Democratic Party chose Bill Scheuerman as its nominee. Bill grew up in Staten Island. He and I met in graduate school at City University's Graduate Center. In 1974, Bill was hired to teach political science at State University of New York, Oswego. At the time, he and his wife Louise had two children with a third on the way. Two years later, I too was hired by the Political Science Department, largely due to Bill's recommendation. We have worked together as close friends ever since. Bill lives in the town of Minetto, which is about five miles south of the city of Oswego and a similar distance north of Fulton. He soon became active in local politics, winning elections both as Town Justice and Town Supervisor, the latter against a long-time Republican incumbent. As a relatively small town squeezed between the county's two cities, however, Minetto has never been very important in county politics.

In 1988 Bill was elected statewide vice-president of the United University Professions (UUP), the union representing faculty and staff of the State University of New York. As a result, he commuted between Albany, where he maintained an apartment, and his house in Minetto, where his family remained. This gave him considerable familiarity with state government but the travel took its toll in inconvenience and strain. We hoped that he would be able to arrange his schedule to work most of the week, then come home for long weekends of campaigning. When Election Day neared, he could use some of his time off to campaign full-time. It would be a real test of his energy.

During the campaign, I kept the journal that follows. In order to maintain the flavor of the campaign, that journal is presented as it was written, except for some editing to improve the writing and eliminate passages that were either repetitive or unimportant. After the journal, a concluding chapter evaluates this particular campaign and addresses some of the larger issues presented in this campaign.

Notes

1. Doris A. Graber, *Mass Media in American Politics,* 3d ed. (Washington, D.C.: CQ Press, 1989), p. 194.

2. John P. Frendreis and Alan R. Gitelson, "Local Political Parties in an Age of Change," *The American Review of Politics,* 14 (Winter 1993), p. 534; and Anthony Gierzynski, *Legislative Party Campaign Committees in the American States* (Lexington, Ky.: University Press of Kentucky, 1992), p. 6.

3. Frank J. Sorauf, *Money in American Elections* (Glenview, Ill.: Scott, Foresman, 1988), p. 260.

4. William Crotty (ed.), *Political Parties in Local Areas* (Knoxville: University of Tennessee Press, 1986); Samuel Eldersveld, *Political Parties: A Behavioral Analysis* (Chicago: Rand McNally, 1964); and Sorauf, 1988, p. 290.

5. Cornelius Cotter, James Gibson, John Bibby, and Robert Huckshorn, *Party Organizations in American Politics* (New York: Praeger, 1984), p. 41.

6. For example, see Martin P. Wattenberg, *The Decline of American Political Parties 1952–1984* (Cambridge, Mass.: Harvard University Press, 1986) and Larry J. Sabato, *The Party's Just Begun* (Glenview, Ill.: Scott, Foresman, 1988).

7. L. Sandy Maisel, *Parties and Elections in America: The Electoral Process* (New York: Random House, 1987), pp. 138–139.

8. Graber, 1989, p. 197; Marjorie Randon Hershey, *Running for Office: The Political Education of Campaigners* (Chatham, N.J.: Chatham House, 1984), chapter 5; and John F. Bibby, "State Party Organizations: Coping and Adapting," in L. Sandy Maisel (ed.), *The Parties Respond*, 2d ed. (Boulder, Colo.: Westview Press, 1994), pp. 21–44.

9. Ruth S. Jones, "Financing State Elections," in Michael Malbin (ed.), *Money and Politics in the United States: Financing Elections in the 1980s* (Chatham, N.J.: Chatham House, 1984), pp. 195–196. See also Paul S. Herrnson, *Party Campaigning in the 1980s* (Cambridge, Mass.: Harvard University Press, 1988), pp. 121–122.

10. For confirmation of this point, see Gierzynski, 1992, pp. 28, 105–107, 111–114; and Joel A. Thompson, William Cassie, and Malcolm E. Jewell, "A Sacred Cow or Just a Lot of Bull? Party and PAC Money in State Legislative Elections," *Political Research Quarterly* 47 (March 1994), pp. 223–237.

11. Cotter et al., 1984, pp. 43–45; and Gibson, Cotter, Bibby, and Huckshorn, "Whither the Local Parties?: A Cross-Sectional and Longitudinal Analysis of the Strength of Party Organizations," *American Journal of Political Science* 29 (Feb. 1985), p. 142.

12. James L. Gibson, John P. Frendreis, and Laura L. Vertz, "Party Dynamics in the 1980s: Change in County Party Organizational Strength, 1980–1984," *American Journal of Political Science* 33 (Feb. 1989), pp. 67–90.

13. Samuel J. Eldersveld, *Political Parties in American Society* (New York: Basic Books, 1982), pp. 199–208.

14. V.O. Key, Jr., *American State Politics* (New York: Knopf, 1956), p. 132; and Cotter et al., 1984, p. 7.

15. John P. Frendreis, James L. Gibson, and Laura L. Vertz, "The Electoral Relevance of Local Party Organizations," *American Political Science Review* 84 (March 1990), pp. 225–235.

16. Gerald M. Pomper, "Party Organizations and Electoral Success," *Polity* 23 (Winter 1990), pp. 187–206; and Robert Huckfeldt and John Sprague, "Political Parties and Electoral Mobilization: Political Structure, Social

Structure and the Party Canvas," *American Political Science Review* 86 (March 1992), pp. 70–86.

17. L. Sandy Maisel, *From Obscurity to Oblivion: Running in the Congressional Primary* (Knoxville: University of Tennessee Press, 1982), pp. 33–34.

18. Hershey, 1984, pp. 61–62.

19. Maisel, 1987, pp. 149–160.

20. Hershey, 1984, pp. 87–92. For an examination of how candidates use polls, see M. Margaret Conway, "The Use of Polls in Congressional, State and Local Elections," *The Annals of the American Academy of Political Science* 472 (March 1984), pp. 97–105. Conway estimates that less than half of state legislative campaigns use polls compared to more than 80 percent of those running for Congress.

21. William J. Crotty, "The Party Organization and Electoral Outcomes," in Crotty, Donald M. Freeman, and Douglas Gatlin (eds.), *Political Parties and Political Behavior*, 2d ed. (Boston: Allyn and Bacon, 1971), p. 302.

22. Susan E. Howell and William S. Oiler, "Campaign Activities and Local Election Outcomes," *Social Science Quarterly* 62 (March 1981), pp. 151–160; and Gerald H. Kramer, "The Effects of Precinct-Level Canvassing on Voter Behavior," *Public Opinion Quarterly* 34 (Winter 1970–1971), pp. 560–572.

23. For a summary of this debate, see Barbara G. Salmore and Stephen A. Salmore, *Candidates, Parties and Campaigns*, 2d ed. (Washington, D.C.: CQ Press, 1989), chapter 1.

24. Gary C. Jacobson, "The Impact of Broadcast Campaigning on Electoral Outcomes," *Journal of Politics* 37 (Aug. 1975), pp. 769–793; and Kent L. Tedin and Richard W. Murray, "Dynamics of Candidate Choice in a State Election," *Journal of Politics* 43 (May 1981), pp. 435–455.

25. Richard Joslyn, *Mass Media and Elections* (Reading, Mass.: Addison-Wesley, 1984), pp. 35–45.

26. For a discussion of how such themes are chosen, see Salmore and Salmore, 1989, chapter 6.

27. Ruth S. Jones, "State and Federal Legislative Campaigns: Same Song, Different Verse," *Election Politics* 3 (Summer 1986), pp. 8–12. See also Jones, 1984, pp. 172–213.

28. Susan E. Howell, "Local Election Campaigns: The Effects of Office Level on Campaign Style," *Journal of Politics* 42 (Nov. 1980), pp. 1135–1145.

29. Sorauf, 1988, p. 261.

30. Like most such definitions, this one is a modified version of David Truman's in *The Governmental Process* (New York: Knopf, 1971), p. 33.

31. V. O. Key, Jr., *Politics, Parties, and Pressure Groups* (New York: Crowell, 1964), p. 18; and Dennis S. Ippolito and Thomas G. Walker, *Political Parties, Interest Groups and Public Policy: Group Influence in American Politics* (Englewood Cliffs, N.J.: Prentice-Hall, 1980), p. 339.

32. Maisel, 1987, p. 88.

33. Allan J. Cigler, "Political Parties and Interest Groups: Competitors, Collaborators, and Uneasy Allies," in Eric M. Uslaner (ed.), *American Political Parties: A Reader* (Itasca, Ill.: F.E. Peacock, 1993), pp. 407–433.

34. Paul E. Peterson, "The Rise and Fall of Special Interest Politics," *Political Science Quarterly* 105 (Winter 1990–91), p. 556.

35. James Madison made this point in *Federalist 10* as a major argument in favor of ratifying the Constitution.

36. Larry J. Sabato, *PAC Power: Inside the World of Political Action Committees* (New York: W. W. Norton, 1985), chapter 3. A recent study confirming this on the state legislative level is Thompson et al., 1994.

37. Sabato, 1985, p. 11.

38. Joslyn, 1984, pp. 153 and 190; and Graber, 1989, p. 209.

39. Robert M. Entman, *Democracy Without Citizens: Media and the Decay of American Politics* (New York: Oxford University Press, 1989), pp. 22–23.

40. Eldersveld, 1982, p. 270.

41. Population statistics are based on 1990 estimates by Donnelly Demographics. Party registration statistics and election results were obtained from the Oswego County Board of Elections.

Campaign Journal

I. INTO THE STARTING BLOCKS

Thursday, May 10

Tonight the endorsement meeting of the Oswego County Democratic Committee was held. Because Bill is in Albany, Louise Scheuerman and I spoke on behalf of his candidacy for Assembly. The party chair, Lou Iorizzo, and I have worked together in the Public Justice Department at school for many years so I knew there would be at least one friendly face at the meeting. Unfortunately, most of the others have never met Bill, putting us at a considerable disadvantage. We do have one thing going for us—a notable lack of enthusiasm for anyone else still in the race. There had been some early speculation that the Mayor of Oswego, John Sullivan, would be a candidate but he declared otherwise earlier today. Bill would not run if either John or Carol Dwyer, an aide to the Assembly speaker, wanted to make the race but Carol had told him that she was unlikely to do so. With the two most formidable party candidates out of the running, and the county chair sympathetic, Bill has a good shot at the party endorsement.

What makes the race intriguing is the incumbent's retirement announcement. Perhaps because of the strongly Republican nature of the district, several candidates have expressed interest in being nominated. This may lead to a primary fight and possibly even a third party run by a disgruntled candidate. At least that is the Democratic party's big hope. With Mario Cuomo at the top of the ticket expected to pull in a lopsided majority, the Democrats see a rare chance to win this Assembly District. Is this wishful thinking? It will be at least a month or two before reality testing.

The meeting began with Lou reading a letter from John Sullivan officially announcing his decision not to run. When a similar announcement from Carol Dwyer was made, several of the committee members made statements wishing she would reconsider. They believed her to be an excellent candidate but everyone knew that her decision not to run was final so another candidate needed to be put forward. In addition to Bill, Bill Maroney and Jim McMahon were at the meeting to express their interest in making the race. Because both had lost previous Assembly races, we hope that the party will turn to someone new. Lou wants Maroney to switch to the State Senate race because no one has expressed interest in running against the incumbent, John McHugh, who looks like an easy winner. The state Democratic party is desperately in search of a candidate to run an energetic race to aid their efforts to add control of the State Senate to the governorship and the Assembly. Even if a Democrat loses this race, it will at least divert resources from nearby districts that look more competitive.

We were glad that the Assembly hopefuls would speak in alphabetical order, giving us a chance to size up the opposition. Maroney spoke very briefly, emphasizing that he is a progressive Democrat who ran a strong race earlier. What was unsaid was that in his previous attempt, he lost a primary and badly divided the party in the November election. There is still considerable resentment about that race, with some people believing that he cost the party a rare chance at victory. McMahon also emphasized his previous run. He had put $20,000 of his own money into it but failed to get as much help from the party as he believed was needed to win. He estimated that victory in this race would cost at least $75,000 to $100,000. In order for him to make the race, he would need a significant monetary contribution from the party. These numbers seemed to stagger nearly everyone present. The Oswego County Democratic party was never very prosperous. It is lucky to raise a few thousand dollars a year for all purposes. Judging from the reaction in the room, McMahon had not helped his prospects.

Now it was my turn. I told the group that I have known Bill for nearly twenty years. He is a dynamic candidate with a proven record. In the town of Minetto, he had defeated the long-time Republican incumbent Town Supervisor by running a strong door-to-door campaign with a budget of $300. He had been interested in the Assembly race, having earlier put together the beginnings of a campaign organization, including some volunteers and a campaign treasurer. When it looked as if either John Sullivan or Carol

Dwyer would run, he decided to step aside for the good of the party and would be happy to do the same should either decide to run. However, with both out of the race, he is prepared to run immediately. Unlike Carol, he has no problems running and keeping his current job as statewide union vice-president. Having worked in Albany for the last two years, much of it on state legislative issues, he would not need much on-the-job training if elected. Louise reinforced my statement, adding some personal notes.

While everything we said was true, there was considerable exaggeration in our description of Bill's organization. We are not sure that his potential campaign treasurer is still available. Nor do we have a huge group of volunteers immediately available but we are confident that we can get some. We appear to have made a good impression but too many people there did not wish to endorse someone whom they had never seen. It was hard to argue with this. We gave out Bill's home number, urging people to call him. Bill has to spend the next week making some calls of his own, introducing himself. On the eighteenth, the party is holding a fundraising dinner that will be Bill's prime exposure. We have done what we could. Now it is up to him.

Sunday, May 13

Bill, Louise, and I sat around their kitchen table planning strategy. Our potential campaign treasurer will be away all summer so we kicked around ideas for a replacement. We also need a campaign manager. Of course, I will do everything possible to help but lack the local connections to be a campaign manager. As a person who was born and raised in New York City and a college professor, Bill needs someone from the area who knows his or her way around rather than another academic from the city. We also went over some names of people who might help out with the campaign or contribute money.

Then we discussed issues. This was a very forbidding subject. Here we were, two apparently well-informed political science professors, realizing how many local issues we need education on. We hope to make jobs a big issue but need to work out some specific programs for this district. Economically, Oswego needs a lot of help, so Bill will work on this. The environment should also be an excellent issue. Voters are very worried about various types of waste dumps that have a tendency to wind up in rural areas like Oswego County. Nearby Cortland has been fighting against a proposed low-level nuclear waste site for which Oswego County was an earlier candidate. We know this has real possibilities since Bill has been fighting on the right side of the issue. Bill is pro-choice on abortion, which we expect to be a plus, but the anti-choice people are very vocal so we have to be prepared for harassment. Bill's experience as an educator and union officer should be an asset in the campaign. We expect to portray him as a fighter for the average person.

Other issues could be more troubling. As two city boys we know very little about the agricultural issues that are of such concern in our district. We have a general sense that the family farm is in trouble and a few ideas but Bill needs a real education here. Some studying and a few trips to visit farmers and discuss their needs would help. The toughest issue for us, however, is likely to be capital punishment. Bill is sympathetic to the governor's opposition but constituency opinion is strongly in favor. We know that if Bill takes a stand against capital punishment, his chances of winning not only the election but even the nomination are in jeopardy. The campaign has not even started and the perennial problem of conscience versus constituency has already surfaced. What compromises must be made to get elected? If other issues are more important to Bill, could he defer to constituents on this one? After all, the current assembly representative, together with virtually all legislators from this part of the state, has voted for the death penalty. Thus, the governor would gain votes on other issues but not lose anything on this one if Bill is elected. I know that this issue will not go away.

Friday, May 18

The JFK Memorial Dinner was a party fund-raiser and Bill's audition. It almost was even more of an audition than we had planned when scheduled speaker Robert Kennedy, Jr., cancelled. Lou replaced him with Andy Spano, one of two Democrats vying to run against State Comptroller Ned Regan, but if Spano could not make it Bill was the back-up speaker. I kept telling him what a great opportunity this would be but suspected that having to write a speech that probably would not be delivered was more pain than pleasure. In fact, it turned out to be a comedy of errors. Bill typed his speech on his laptop computer but, not having a printer, stopped by to use mine. Before printing, he decided to make a few changes, somehow managing to delete his entire speech from the computer's memory during the process. Of course, he had neither made a back-up copy nor written it down, which meant he had to return home to reconstruct and retype the speech. A few hours later he was back with a version that he claimed was less eloquent than the original. This time he decided to print without making any changes and our apparently simple task was performed. It is a good thing for his constituents that if elected he will be able to hire people to take care of anything that relates to a computer.

The dinner started with cocktails at 6:30. Because Spano's plane was delayed, Bill remained on standby. Quite a few people approached me and Louise to tell us what a good job we had done at the committee meeting last week. Louise seemed pleased to hear this but I, being a somewhat cynical academic, dismissed it as possibly sincere but more likely standard political flattery. After all, what politician would tell me what a lousy speech I had given? We introduced everyone to Bill, who did his best to circulate among the eighty or ninety people present. Such a good turnout pleased those attending but the group was small enough for Bill to speak to everyone. Spano showed up near the end of the dinner, leading Bill to breathe the proverbial sigh of relief. The three Assembly hopefuls were introduced after the main speech to say a few words about themselves.

Spano's speech was fairly well received. After telling some good anecdotes, he launched into a lecture on pension and fiscal management. My own view is that he will be hard-pressed to win the likely primary against Carol Bellamy, let alone beat Regan. After Spano's speech, the Assembly candidates again spoke in alphabetical order. For some reason, Maroney decided to make a speech in support of the city annexing several college dorms that are part of the town of Oswego. No one could figure out what this had to do with the Assembly race and Maroney went on at so much length that Lou had to remind him to keep it short. McMahon did much better, briefly stating his qualifications and hopes. Bill was nervous about going up but did very well. He was the only one of the three who actually invoked JFK, the supposed theme of the dinner. He got in some of his own qualifications while poking a bit of fun at himself by saying how hard it is for someone who is both a politician and a college professor to be brief but he managed it. He hopes to use the social concern of a John Kennedy to replace the aid to the rich that has been the concern of the Republicans in Washington.

We are optimistic that Bill made a good impression. The reporters at the dinner agreed. One told him that it is about time for a new face and gave him her card. The Republicans have endorsed their candidate, Frances Sullivan, whose prime qualification seems to be that she is the widow of a judge. None of us is aware of any other qualifications she has or of her positions on the issues. We speculate that she has been chosen as the least controversial candidate to avoid factional fighting.

Thursday, May 24

This should have been a week of furious activity; instead it was as if time had frozen. Because the Democratic committee originally planned to make an endorsement two weeks ago, we expected to know by now. Instead, their plan seems to be to hope that all possible candidates but one will drop out, thereby avoiding a primary fight. With a strategy like this, running the risk of turning three candidates into none, it is no wonder that the Democrats frequently fail to give the Republicans serious opposition.

Bill is out there politicking away. Today he went to the Fulton Democrats' spaghetti supper. According to his account, he sat with two very square jawed state troopers and their wives. Then he did his bit, going from table to table to get acquainted. He seems to have survived in good cheer, which augurs well for a campaign that will be filled with such events. The media age has not revolutionized Oswego county politics. Here you win your votes a few at a time by going to dinners and picnics, knocking on doors, and making speeches to small groups. The county contains no major media markets so that a television ad in Syracuse, which is outside the district, would be largely wasted money, money that most candidates for Assembly cannot afford. Media means radio and newspapers. If Bill wins the nomination, we will have to work on some radio ads and work even harder to get out press releases and call news conferences. I hope we can raise enough money to do some early polling but am not very optimistic. With a little luck we might be able to get some help, in money or in services, from the state committee. With even more luck we could attract a couple of big-time political figures to generate coverage by the local media and possibly one of the Syracuse TV stations.

Local newspaper coverage of last week's dinner was decent, concentrating primarily on Spano's speech with a paragraph on the three Assembly possibilities and their backgrounds. One picture in the *Oswego Valley News* lined up the three, together with the Democratic candidate for Fulton city court judge. If the party ever picks someone, at least the name and face will be familiar to a few voters. Tomorrow Bill will call Jim McMahon to try to work out an accommodation.

Wednesday, June 6

Two more weeks have passed with no moves by the local party to make an endorsement. Lou attended the state convention, which surprised no one by nominating Mario Cuomo for another term as governor, Robert Abrams as attorney general, and putting both Andy Spano and Carol Bellamy on the primary ballot for comptroller. The big surprise was how harmonious the normally contentious Democrats were while the Republicans battled over abortion after finally finding a gubernatorial candidate in economist Pierre Rinfret. I ran into Lou at the bank this morning and asked him when the party was going to endorse a candidate for assembly. To my surprise he told me that they would meet tomorrow evening. Bill is in Washington but Lou and I will try to get Louise to make sure Bill shows up (he is due back tonight). According to Lou, Bill should get the nod at the meeting if he appears and does as well as he has so far. He has generated some enthusiasm in contrast to the other hopefuls.

This was a modest surprise compared to what happened next. At 3:30 Bill called from Washington, D.C., with the sudden announcement that he is out of the race. He had seen a doctor who told him that he has a mild ulcer that could be controlled by diet and minimizing stress. He had also gotten some criticism from other union officials who do not share the president's enthusiasm for Bill's running for assembly while keeping his union job. Unfortunately, at long distance rates there was not much time for discussion. Bill tends to be very passionate in his beliefs and sensitive to problems, which is why he has an ulcer and why he sometimes needs people to keep him on an even keel. It also makes him a fighter and a doer, the image we want to present to the public.

On a personal level, however, it occasionally makes life difficult for family and friends. Even though he is not yet officially a candidate, he has already changed his mind about running numerous times. Usually, Louise and I patiently remind him of how often he has been unduly discouraged in the past, ask him to think about it, and wait for the mood to pass. In a long political campaign, ups and downs are to be expected so a candidate needs people to raise his spirits in his low moods as well as prevent him from taking positive signs too seriously. Unfortunately, this time he sounded more serious than usual. I talked to him about changing his patterns of thinking to take setbacks more lightly. He promised to call me when he got home to talk things over.

Louise called about an hour and a half later. "What did you hear about Bill?" she asked. We have known each other long enough for me to understand that she knew something that I didn't. "Exactly what do you want to know?" I dead-panned. After stringing me along for a bit, she told all: Bill was running. What about his ulcer, the objections from the union, etc.? He would take care of them. They are going to the endorsement meeting tomorrow. I need to be prepared for these kind of shocks. In the long run they will mean little but if Bill is to have a chance we will have to modify his highs and lows.

Then we discussed details. Louise will help with finances. She is good with money and we could hardly think of someone more trustworthy. I repeated the reasons I gave earlier for not being campaign manager. I would do as much work as possible but suggested a few names of local people with better connections to the nonacademic community. I added some other ideas. Bill has frequently complained about supermarket scanners. Since most local supermarkets that use them fail to comply with the law requiring them to put prices on individual items, we should get in touch with the Attorney General's office to see if someone could come to town to hold a news conference outside a supermarket that has violated the law but received minimal or no fines. Bill could then suggest toughening the penalties. This will be a good issue that Bill feels strongly about. By attacking supermarket chains, we are not likely to alienate local business people. We might even bring in the local unions by doing this at a nonunion store. I also suggested getting in touch with the newly chosen Democratic senate candidate who neither of us knows. Scheduling some joint appearances could help both candidates.

At 10:30 Bill called in an upbeat mood. He had given a talk to a group consisting primarily of rural women who had not recognized his name but remembered his face from the time several years ago that he helped them fight against the power company. Although the waste issue had energized and angered them, their experience had given them reason not to trust the Republicans. Because they knew Bill had been on their side in the past, several volunteered to work for him. Suddenly Bill has good reason to be optimistic. Nancy Larraine Hoffman captured a nearby state senate seat from an incumbent Republican several years ago and has managed to retain it in large part because of the loyal support of farmers. Usually the strategy of a Democratic candidate in this district is to roll up majorities in the cities of Oswego and Fulton. However, the few who have been able to do this found it insufficient to overcome larger Republican majorities in the towns and rural areas. If Bill can cut into the farm vote he has a chance. A college professor born and raised in New York City would not seem to be a good prospect for doing this, but the waste issue could help. Not only is Bill's position closer to that of most voters than his opponent's, but also he has the record to back it up, having attended numerous demonstrations in the past when he had nothing to gain. Perhaps doing the right thing would pay off.

What happened to the problems that were going to make him withdraw? He spoke with Nuala Drescher, a former UUP President and still a power in the union, who urged him to run. The ulcer is mild and is something Bill will have to live with no matter what. I reminded him of the possible strains of a political campaign—he will be attacked and misquoted by the opposition, by hecklers, and by the media. You cannot take these things too seriously but have to deal with them as effectively as possible and move on. Bill agreed, but I know this is a message that will have to be delivered again when the situation warrants. Otherwise, we discussed some mundane details that had to be taken care of such as the three-person vacancy committee needed for the petitions required to get on the ballot (I agreed to serve) and an announcement of candidacy for a press conference, should he get the party's endorsement. Our first big decision day is tomorrow.

Thursday, June 7

The endorsement meeting turned out to be pleasantly anticlimactic. Although it was supposed to start at 7:30, people took their time coming, leaving us the opportunity to chat and get acquainted with those we had not yet met. One was the state senate candidate, Margaret Pavel. The senate district is huge, spreading from the southern end of Oswego county where she is from to northern New

York, including Watertown and Potsdam. Bill promised to help get her in touch with people he knows at SUNY Potsdam. Margaret seemed to be a nice person with a great deal of enthusiasm for the race. She had gotten the call to head to Albany for the party convention and rushed off to be on the platform with the other Democratic challengers to Republican incumbents. The statewide strategy seems to have as many women as possible run, stressing family issues such as day care and protection of children as well as taking a pro-choice stand on abortion. Running against an incumbent who has done nothing to alienate anyone in a strongly Republican district, Margaret is at best a long shot.

A single parent with two young children, little financial support, and virtually no name recognition, she is hardly the candidate a computer would choose but everyone present was quite pleased. She has been a party committee member since 1974, is energetic and excited about running, and has taken positions on the issues that the party is very comfortable with. Bill discussed working with her as well as arranging as many joint appearances as possible. After attendance was taken, Lou introduced Margaret, allowing her to make a brief statement. She was unanimously endorsed. While this was going on, I was thinking of the comment in Frank Sorauf and Paul Beck's textbook on political parties that "the local party organization typically is a weak organizational force in the community, with the real leadership more generally assumed by the party's elected public officials." From my quick count, more than half of the committee members were unrepresented and many of the others had sent in proxies. The party's two major elected officials, the mayors of Oswego and Fulton, were not present. A full slate of loyal party candidates would make this meeting a huge success. No one present could remember the last time the party put forth a full slate of candidates.

Bill, Louise, and I kept looking around for his competitors but neither had shown up. Apparently the strategy of waiting for the field to reduce itself had worked. Lou read a brief statement from Jim McMahon announcing his withdrawal and wishing the nominee good luck. Even though Bill Maroney was also apparently out, there was some talk that he would seek the Liberal nomination out of pique against the mayor. While he would be unlikely to get many votes, most would come from Bill. Committee members were angry, having seen Maroney run such a divisive race once before. Fortunately, attention now turned to Bill. Both Carol Dwyer and the Minetto contingent nominated him. Because they had been so nice about it, Bill thanked them after the meeting. He was introduced and made a brief statement about his background, his goals in running, and his bluntness. Not everyone agrees with him on all issues but there is no doubt about where he stands. He too was endorsed by acclamation. If only the voters are as receptive as the committee people. Lou had also found a candidate for county sheriff, Jerry Herrington. A muscular guy wearing dark glasses, Jerry looked like a sheriff. While no public speaker, he expressed some criticisms of the incumbent. When asked about a previous sheriff, Ray Miller, he told the audience that Ray, who converted to the Democratic party several years ago, would back him. Another unanimous endorsement followed. Because the party actually had willing candidates for all offices but county clerk, the meeting was considered a success.

Geraldine Ferraro has expressed an interest in speaking at a party fund-raiser. It is common knowledge that she is testing the climate for a 1992 U.S. Senate race. Before taking any action Lou wanted to consult with the party. As a marquee name she would raise a lot of money and generate quite a bit of publicity. However, the only comment came from someone who did not want her. He insisted that she had hurt the party with her run for vice-president.

Campaign button (blue and white)

"If only she hadn't run," I whispered to Bill, "Mondale would have won easily." No chance that I would ever be a candidate with such a sarcastic attitude. With no additional comments the decision was deferred.

The meeting was over but our work was not. After Bill thanked everyone, I introduced him to Jack Tyrie, whom I have suggested as a possible campaign manager. Jack is a teacher in Hannibal who played a prominent role in Norma Bartle's campaign for state senate the year John McHugh was first elected. Because Norma's husband taught in our department at Oswego, we had followed that race very closely. With good local connections, Jack seems to me to be a natural to run Bill's campaign. The two of them agreed to get together soon to discuss what role Jack would play in the campaign.

Bill has also prepared a press release to announce his candidacy. The original version read too much like a resume so I suggested some ways of punching it up. Instead of leading off with his experience, the new version starts with a statement of why he wants to run. I like the new version, but we plan to wait a few days before releasing it. There was a reporter present at the endorsement meeting taking photos for a story. We decided to hold the announcement until after the story appears. With our low-budget campaign, we want to turn the endorsement and the announcement of candidacy into two stories, hoping that the second will get wider coverage than the first.

"Am I crazy to do this?" Bill asked me. I repeated my usual football analogy. "If you got a chance to try out for the Giants and didn't take it, wouldn't you regret it for the rest of your life? If you tried out, the worst that would happen would be that the other players would beat you up and laugh at you but at least you would know that you tried." Bill, a true Giants fanatic, always appreciated this analogy. What I did not tell him is that in politics there are no referees, no substitutes to relieve him, and no time-outs. For us training camp is over. A very long season is about to begin.

II. OFF AND RUNNING

Friday, June 8

First on the agenda was a meeting with the college president, Steve Weber. Since Bill's election would give the college as good a friend as possible in a legislature that has few members who are even SUNY alumni, we expected a friendly meeting, which is what Bill got. Steve was very sympathetic to Bill's candidacy and promised that, should he win the election, there would be little problem in getting an unpaid leave.

The rest of the day was for the news media. All the local newspapers and radio stations wanted interviews. With our limited budget we made sure that every media outlet, no matter how small, got one. At this early stage, getting exposure and favorable name recognition is our main goal. Bill and I have spoken numerous times about what image he should try to project. My advice is to convey the picture of a fighter for the average person in the district. Such an image emphasizes Bill's strengths and minimizes his weaknesses. It is a pretty accurate if oversimplified picture of who he really is. It highlights his own experience as a union leader and town supervisor as well as his pre-graduate school work as a parole officer and train engineer. It demonstrates that he will not simply be a puppet of the party leadership. On major issues such as jobs, reproductive rights, the environment, education, and consumer rights, it shows in a shorthand way just what he will do. It also presents a good contrast to his opponent, who was chosen by insiders and who lacks a record like Bill's. When constituents disagree with him, he will speak forthrightly (as long as he does not disagree with them too often, of course), proving that disagreement about an issue or two will not stop him from battling aggressively for them.

The interviews went well. Excerpts from the radio tapes were run almost hourly on the news. Bill got across our major themes, emphasizing that the previous assemblyman, while a very nice fellow, had been unable to do much as a member of the minority party in an Assembly dominated by the Democrats. Bill will aggressively "bring home the bacon" to the district while not hesitating to express disagreement with his party leaders when the district's interests require it. One of the radio stations balanced this with an interview with his opponent who said that she would work quietly within the system to get things done rather than take strong public positions. This delighted us as it is just the sort of contrast we are looking for. We think that the public is tired of politics as usual and is looking for an upfront person like Bill to represent them. Our one serious problem is capital punishment. Bill shrewdly ducked the issue by telling reporters that he will have a position paper on crime soon, detailing his stand on all crime-related issues including the death penalty. As a result, none of the radio interviews used this issue but, if Bill is to be as honest and upfront as he has pictured himself, he will have to take a stand soon.

Saturday, June 9

Tomorrow we will have a meeting of those people we expect to be most active in the campaign. Because I am the person whose judgment Bill trusts the most—though I have no formal title—I will have the final word on press releases and other statements as well as strategic decisions. Of course, I will not do anything that Bill would disapprove of. We have been so close for so many years that it is easy for me to know just what he thinks and what he would and would not agree with. The one exception will be those local issues that I simply have little background on. For them I will defer to those who know what they are talking about.

At tomorrow's meeting we will discuss capital punishment. I asked Bill just what his conscience tells him. He answered that it would be very hard for him to be in favor of capital punishment. I suggested two possible options. If he cannot compromise at all, he should take a strong position against capital punishment but not bring it up unless asked. We know that he will be asked quite frequently so he needs a response that will not be too complicated. The classes on the subject I have taught have made me pretty knoweldgeable about it. I proposed the following approach. First of all, it is a matter of conscience. Like Governor Cuomo he does not believe it is right for the state to take a life, no matter how evil the criminal. He could never live with himself if, after someone was executed, it was discovered that person was innocent. Second, most people wrongly think the death penalty would save money. However, Kansas rejected capital punishment partly because of a study showing that it would cost $50 million and probably take ten years before anyone was executed. In a time of budgetary crisis, we can hardly afford such wasteful expenditures nor should we sentence people to death, then wait for them to die of old age while the court system grinds slowly along. Third, he supports the governor's proposal of life without parole. New York's fragmented court system has caused too many delays, allowed too many plea bargains, and wasted too much money; so he supports streamlining the courts to make them more efficient. This would free up more money for more useful expenditures. I also suggested some ways to increase the number of police and improve their training to bring them more into line with twenty-first century needs.

Although Bill was impressed with these arguments, I pointed out that they would do no more than mitigate some of the damage. Opposing capital punishment will cost him votes no matter how convincing the two of us found these points. The voters tend to give a governor more room to oppose them on matters of conscience than their legislators who they expect to reflect their views on major issues. Several recent murder cases in the district have even resulted in judges saying they wish the death penalty could be imposed. In one case, a fugitive from murder charges in Florida hid in the house of some people on vacation. A high school student agreed to feed his neighbors' dog while they were away. Unfortunately, he surprised the fugitive and was brutally murdered. During the trial, the family and many of the friends of the popular boy made emotional pleas for the death penalty. It is quite obvious that sentiment for capital punishment in the district is overwhelming.

Could Bill in good conscience support the death penalty in any way? Perhaps, he said, but only in an extremely limited fashion. This led me to propose option two. Bill could support the death penalty for murderers who kill while trying to escape from prison and for incorrigible serial killers. He could then stress that the death penalty can only reduce crime if it is part of a comprehensive approach, allowing him to bring in some of the proposals from option one. My suggestion for an attention-catching proposal was a New York State Police Corps. College students would be given scholarships if they agree to join a police department for at least four years. This would enable the police to attract high-quality officers, increase the number of police, and help the educational system all at once. It would be very consistent with Bill's campaign themes. My proposal was not terribly original (a federal version was pending in Congress), but Bill liked it and thought it would go over well with voters.

I cautioned that option two has its dangers. Bill will inevitably face the question of whether his position would allow him to vote for the death penalty bill that the governor has vetoed every year. The logical answer would be that the proposal has changed some from year to year so that Bill's vote would depend upon just what was in it. However, this answer is unlikely to satisfy voters, and would take away from Bill's image of forthrightness.

In 1774, Edmund Burke told the Electors of Bristol that as their representative he owed them "his judgment; and he betrays, instead of serving you, if he sacrifices it to your opinion." Since that time, philosophers, political scientists, and occasionally even politicians have debated whether such a view of representation is consistent with democracy. It is a debate that I have often led in the classroom. Here is a chance to apply what we have learned and taught in real life. An election could turn on our decision.

Sunday, June 10

Our first campaign committee meeting presented an interesting group of people. Present in addition to Bill, Louise, and me were Nancy Weber and Marie Austin, two of the women Bill met at the meeting last week; Ray Peterson and John Wilson, two of our former students; Dave Turner, head of the local labor council; Greg Auleta, president of our campus UUP chapter; and Lois Peterson, a close friend of Louise's. Nancy is a farmer and Marie an environmental activist who has worked against incinerators and waste dumps and has started a recycling project. Ray teaches at Jefferson Community College in Watertown, which is outside the district, but he lives within it and his family comes from Mexico, which is located in Oswego County. John sells insurance and has lived in the county all his life. Both of their families are quite politically active. It is a reasonably diverse group with connections in many parts of the district that neither Bill nor I have. In addition, because we agree on major issues there is not likely to be much friction.

It was time to get to work on details. I volunteered to get past voting statistics broken down by city and town. We came up with some fund-raising ideas, then tried to divide up responsibilities. With some twenty towns in Oswego County, we hope to set up liaisons with one or two contacts in each. Lois is in charge of scheduling, and all events that we think Bill should attend will be cleared through her. We already have a few including the anniversary of a country music station (Bill is a country music fan so this should go over well), meetings of environmental groups, and picnics. Bill knows of a band that will play for a benefit if we can find a place to hold it. Dave knows the chair of the Assembly Agriculture Committee, who might be willing to come to the district. There are a number of endorsements we think we can get, so our hope is to announce one a week to keep up a steady flow of good news in the media. For example, we expect many labor unions to support Bill. Jim McMahon also promised to help. Since he lives in the town of Hastings, not a place where our contacts are strong, anything he can do for us will be a big plus. We already talked to Paul Austin, the president of the college's Student Association, who agreed to help register students. Greg and I will distribute a fund-raising letter to faculty.

Bill is also going to meet with John Sullivan for help in raising money. We know we can get an endorsement from John. He is the best known political figure in the city, but he has made a few enemies. As for the state party, it has promised some money and other support if Bill can demonstrate that he is doing well. Since we need money to do well, this has the potential of becoming a vicious circle. But Bill has a plan. He will have campaign material printed up and billed to the local party, which he will repay when the state party's money comes in. I wonder whether, with such a head for fiscal gimmickry, Bill's talents belong at the federal level.

We then turned to issues. There are a lot of good ideas in this group. On some issues Bill needs briefings to fill him in on the local angles. Nancy and Marie are particularly good, but Ray and John are also knowledgeable. Louise knows quite a bit about welfare and poverty while Dave is the local labor expert. I brought up the subject of capital punishment. After considerable soul searching Bill has decided against supporting the death penalty. He then started bringing up the arguments and statistics I had given him earlier. No need to convince us, I replied, then suggested that he also might say something like, "As a former parole officer I am not sentimental about criminals but I could not live with myself if even one in a hundred or one in a thousand people executed turned out to be innocent. I believe that there are many other things we can do about crime." Then he could move into his anti-crime suggestions. Everyone liked this argument but I pointed out that it is only damage control and that the issue will surely cost us votes. Greg concurred, pointing to the same case I had mentioned earlier. Nevertheless, we all agreed that if it costs us the election, so be it.

Overall, however, it was an upbeat meeting. None of us has much experience in running political campaigns but each of us brings other types of important experience or knowledge. We have a good core group that will meet every two weeks during the summer, then more often after Labor Day. Jack Tyrie, who Bill and I hope will be our official campaign manager, was out of town. But Bill left some messages on his answering machine. Carol Dwyer could not make this meeting but will come in the future. Even I, a pessimist by nature, am beginning to feel that we have a reasonable chance of victory. I remind myself that I need to be the realist of the group, but this is not the time for such thoughts.

Thursday, June 14

I have been away at the Shaw Festival in Canada. I enjoyed a few days of theater, watching no television and reading only Canadian newspapers but now it is back to reality. Most of Bill's news is good. He has scheduled as many events as possible, working in Albany during the week and then returning for long weekends of appearances. This weekend, for example, in addition to meeting with various politicians, he is going to the Strawberry Festival and the country music station's anniversary. The latter has turned out to be particularly important because that radio station is owned by an active Republican who has given Democratic candidates as little coverage as possible. Some money has begun to come in, with a number of contributions of fifty dollars or more, including two hundred dollars from John Wilson. Such contributions would not even be worth noting for the large campaigns I sometimes write about, but for us they have provided necessary seed money. John has been working as well as we could have hoped, contacting lots of people. As I had suggested, Bill wrote a fund-raising letter to faculty and staff that Greg and I will distribute. Bill has also printed up some palm cards so we now will have something to give away. I suggested we also get bumper stickers (everyone drives in this district so they will be very visible) and T-shirts.

Jack Tyrie was happy to take the job as campaign manager. Lou had been pressing him to manage Margaret Pavel's Senate campaign but this one has more of a chance of winning (perhaps I should say this one has a chance of winning) and is in a smaller district. The Senate district is huge, going way up north while the Assembly district is only Oswego County. Jack and I will get together soon to plot strategy. The few times we have met we have gotten on well. Because he knows the district so much better than I do and has had some experience, albeit in losing campaigns, we should complement each other well.

Bill got past election results that depressed him somewhat. The best starting point for us was the 1980 election that first elected the current Assemblyman, Ray Chesbro. The Democratic candidate, Mike Yerdon, ran a pretty good race but was swamped. Looking at those returns, Bill wondered whether he really has a chance but I was able to offer an optimistic interpretation on these figures. First of all, I told him to look at the top of the ticket. Cuomo against Rinfret looks a lot better than Carter versus Reagan. Second, the opposition was weaker. Chesbro had been a widely known and admired former sheriff while Frances Sullivan was a political unknown, handpicked by the Republican party leaders. Third, in 1980 students had been prevented from voting in the district, but now there are no extra hurdles, and there is even an on-campus election district. We need to work with the Student Association (SA) on a voter registration drive and Bill, who has not taught for three years, has to make some appearances before student groups. Students have always liked him, and his positions on most issues are far more in accord with theirs than his opponent's. We need to take advantage of the SA president's promise to help. Fourth, Yerdon had changed parties after his defeat and we have been told that he hoped to gain the nomination this year. After the Republican leaders ignored him, he decided both to contest the nomination and run on an independent ticket. Such a run might take some votes from Bill but should siphon off far more from his opponent, especially since Bill has been circulating petitions to add an independent ballot line to the Democratic one. I suggested that with three candidates, we could win with 12,000 to 14,000 votes. Bill, Jack, and I will look at the county to see how to add up the votes to get there. I believe that if we can mobilize Bill's natural vote, get his name across well enough to add some independents and disgruntled Republicans, and do well in debating Sullivan (who we do not expect to be nearly as good at debates as Bill, who is very articulate and quick on his feet as befits a good teacher), we will have a good chance of winning.

It would be nice if we could convince the state party people of this in order to induce them to give us some money but they want a poll taken in July. They would supply a pollster who would look at the district; design a questionnaire; and provide instructions to our volunteers who would then make four hundred calls from a phone bank that we would pay for. Having written quite a bit on how polls are used in politics, I know that such a poll would be of little use to us. Using volunteers to take a poll adds to the possible error—they are inexperienced, will likely have a very short training session, and may communicate their own beliefs to the people being interviewed. A poll taken this early in a campaign pitting two relative newcomers against each other would surely show that neither candidate has much support. Most voters would be undecided and unable to communicate much about the candidates. Still, the poll could be of some value. Any information about issues and about the distribution within the district of potential supporters (although this will be a bit tricky with a sample this small) would complement what we already know. In addition, if the poll does show low support for our opponent (even if it is also low for Bill), coupled with a very large undecided vote, it could provide a basis for arguing that we can win. If so, perhaps we could parlay the few hundred dollars it will cost us into some cash from the state party.

Oswego Mayor John Sullivan has agreed to turn over his fundraising list, which we need badly. He also has made some worthwhile suggestions. His considerable political experience has the potential to help us a great deal.

Friday, June 15

Bill went to a local attorney to have some minor changes made in his will. This attorney, a Republican, said to Bill, "Give me a dollar." "Sure," replied Bill, "what kind of raffle are you selling?" Instead of a raffle, he got back $50. Since we do not have to give the names of contributors of less than $100, the attorney does not have to worry about his Republican associates who expect him to work for Frances Sullivan. He promised to vote for Bill and quietly lobby some of his friends to do the same. He also told Bill that Sullivan opposes abortion except in cases of danger to the pregnant woman's life or rape or incest. From our point of view this position, although consistent with that of many voters, is a plus. It will cost her the Right to Life Party's support. At the same time, we can draw a contrast between her view and Bill's pro-choice position. We hope to get the pro-choice vote while the right-to-lifers go for Yerdon or stay home. The Republicans are particularly vulnerable on this issue because the national party platform has been strongly against all abortions except to save the life of the woman while the state party only recently changed its platform to become pro-choice, the stance taken by its gubernatorial candidate. I urged Bill to ask his opponent during debates and at all other possible opportunities which Republican platform she agrees with—the national party, the current state party, or last month's state party. Since her position is different from all three, I expect that the contradiction will cause her real problems.

Sunday, June 17

Our first weekend of real campaigning. For the next few months Bill will be working most of the week in Albany, then commuting home for long weekends of campaign activity. Yesterday he went to Pulaski for WSCP's anniversary celebration. It took a great deal of persistence to get them to agree to let him speak but, since his opponent had been invited, they really had little choice. He was able to stay on the air for about fifteen minutes by saying something on the order of "We're having a great time here so come on down," whenever the host made a move to the microphone, leading to another question. The basic theme was a variation on what he has been saying, that he will be an independent voice, working with the majority but fighting the party leadership when the district's needs are not being met. When asked about his big-city origins, he replied, as he has steadily done, that he lives in Oswego County "by choice not by chance." He also pointed out that the Republican party can no longer be counted on to look after upstate because its center of gravity, as evidenced in its gubernatorial candidate and Senate majority leader, has shifted to New York City and Long Island. After speaking, he mingled with the crowd, chatting briefly with everyone and giving out our newly printed cards with his picture and a couple of lines of text emphasizing his fighting spirit. All in all, a successful appearance.

In the evening it was on to a Catholic church bazaar in downtown Oswego. This was a less successful appearance simply because we got to fewer people. Bill, Louise, and I knew only a small number of those present, which meant that Bill had to introduce himself and then make his pitch. All things considered, he did this pretty well but still has a long way to go to master what Robert Caro, referring to Lyndon Johnson, called "the amazing talent for meeting and greeting," for establishing rapport with total strangers with apparent spontaneity. Early events like this will be a good training ground. We gingerly avoided the area near the prolife booth, concentrating on the food areas. Among those we knew were Monsignor Furfaro who, in addition to his church office, is chair of the College Council and a member of the Board of Education; and Tina Piericcini from the college's Communications Studies Department, who volunteered to recruit one of her students as an intern.

Today was also the Strawberry Festival. John Wilson did a great job taking Bill around. John has that knack for going up to

The candidate and his wife (*center*) meeting voters in Oswego County.

people and getting acquainted quickly. He then introduces Bill to his new friend. Several of the farmers were particularly impressed by Bill's knowledge of their problems, something he acquired in an excellent briefing by Nancy Weber. One even offered 1,100 feet of farm space bordering on a main road for putting up signs. We hope that Bill's mild but obvious Staten Island accent will not hurt.

Monday, June 18

While Bill met with Jack Tyrie, Greg and I distributed our faculty fund-raising letter. Signed by the two of us, it stresses the importance of having a strong advocate for SUNY in the legislature in light of the yearly budget fights. It also includes a coupon to send in with a contribution or a declaration of willingness to volunteer. Although it is summertime, Wednesday is payday so we expect quite a few people coming in to pick up their checks to read our appeal. With no mailing costs, even a small return will be a success. Greg has also contacted a local entrepreneur about donating a concert hall for a fund-raiser. We will keep what we charge for admission if Larry is able to sell drinks for his share.

Bill and Jack seem to get along well. Even though he too is originally from downstate, Jack knows the district well, has considerable campaign experience, and has made some excellent suggestions. One is to run a biographical ad on two local radio stations during the summer to help build name recognition. On WSGO, Oswego's main station, a minimum of ten ads would cost seven dollars each. Bill's new favorite station, WSCP in Pulaski, has similarly low rates. Producing the ad ourselves would not cost much and it could be reused during the fall campaign. Even our budget allows such a media blitz!

Sunday, June 24

A relatively quiet weekend. On Friday I was interviewed about my forthcoming book, *LBJ and the Polls*, by a former student of mine who does a public affairs program for a local rock radio station. Tim will call Bill to arrange an interview soon. The program airs 6:30 Sunday morning, not exactly prime time, but it is free and every little bit helps. Bill has kept up his series of appearances, attending the Fulton Farmers' Market yesterday and a Hibernians' breakfast this morning. Next weekend is Oswego's Fourth of July parade. Because this is one of the year's biggest local events, we will have our own float with as many people as possible wearing the "Scheuerman for Assembly" T-shirts that Louise is ordering. The parade's large attendance guarantees substantial media coverage, usually attracting the Syracuse television stations. Just having a large crowd see us will be great but getting on TV would be a huge bonus. These are the stations that the entire county views.

We have made progress in raising money, although dollar totals in the hundreds look small to someone used to more high-tech campaigns. Louise will continue to do most of the financial record-keeping but we decided that she needs some help. Fortunately, Greg volunteered. This will take away a few worries from Louise, who is quite anxious whenever there is a possibility of something going wrong (which is frequent and likely to get worse). Our campus fund-raising appeal has started a trickle of funds. Bill also went to our first small group fund-raiser in Palermo. The idea is to have a local person host a gathering of friends and pass a fishbowl to collect small contributions. With so many remote towns in the district, we hope this will eventually raise a bit of money as well as help to recruit volunteers. Outside of endorsing Bill and promising to get the five hundred petition signatures that we need to get on the ballot, the party has done little to promote Bill's candidacy. Lou is now claiming that he cannot find any place in the county to have a fund-raiser with Geraldine Ferraro, which will force him to have it in Watertown. This is such an absurd claim that we do not know what to make of it but moving the fund-raiser so far north would really hurt us. We have so little confidence in the party that one of Louise's sources of worry is that they will fail to get us on the ballot. I told her not to worry since we could watch them carefully and, if necessary, get the signatures ourselves. Our even having to think about such things, however, is a sad commentary on the state of the local party organization.

Monday, June 25

Tonight Bill, Louise, Jack Tyrie, John Wilson, and I got together for a two-hour strategy meeting. Bill's schedule calls for three or four days per week at his job in Albany (summer is a slow time, so he should get a couple of weeks of vacation time as well). As a result, we have been able to arrange events for virtually every weekend for the next month and a half, with more to come. Bill likes going to them with John so that they have become an informal traveling team. Jack has begun to put out a flurry of press releases on our newly printed stationery, one for each event, generally with a statement by Bill stressing one of our campaign themes. We expect a reasonable amount of publicity to result, especially later in the electoral season when the campaign becomes more newsworthy. We also arranged coordinators for most of the towns in the county. Our plan is to concentrate on the towns along the Oswego River and the western part of the district as well as the cities of Oswego and Fulton. We looked at past election results as well as our own experience to this point to help us target. A high-tech campaign would have taken a poll or two but we do not have much confidence in the poll that the state party will be arranging. Bill will try to get to all parts of the district but our mailings, advertising, and most of his appearances will be in the targeted areas. This week's events include the Independence Day parade in Oswego, the very big air show in Fulton, and an ice cream social in Mexico.

On issues, Bill's luck in avoiding the capital punishment issue will not last much longer. He has begun to consider the possibility of acceding to the wishes of the voters and supporting the death penalty. The position I had worked out was to state simply that this most extreme penalty is necessary for the most extreme cases without being too specific about those extreme cases. Bill will give this some consideration but for now thinks it is a position he could, pardon the awful pun, live with. He could counterattack by arguing that if the governor's veto of the death penalty is sustained, the legislature ought to vote life without parole for the worst convicted murderers. The Republicans' failure to do this despite widespread public support is largely a tactic to put political heat on Cuomo. We are also going to make a push for family issues such as parental leave and more day care. Local concern over a variety of waste disposal programs—incinerators, low level nuclear wastes, and chemical dumps—are a natural for us. Bill and Nancy Weber are also working on some farm issues.

Organizationally our biggest minus has become the county Democratic Party. Jack discovered that messages on the party's answering machine are from as far back as June 6. One of them had been from the National Education Association asking about the party's assembly candidate in order to distribute a questionnaire to use for their endorsement. Because NEA is potentially a strong source of support for us, missing this opportunity would have been a huge blow to our campaign. Fortunately Jack called them quickly, described Bill's position on education issues, and discovered that their candidate interviews will be this Friday. We will quickly pick up and fill out a questionnaire, then clear time for Bill to go to Liverpool (a suburb of Syracuse) for their interview.

In case this was not damaging enough, we have a problem with Lou. When the press asked him about a possible Republican primary between Sullivan and Yerdon he actually stated that the Democrats hoped that Sullivan would win to give us a better chance! If Bill is asked such a question he will stay out of Republican politics, instead saying that he plans a positive campaign stressing his positions on the issues and looks forward to running against whomever the Republicans choose. Pretty bland stuff directly from the politicians' cliché book, but with good reason. This will be a difficult enough campaign without giving the Republicans extra ammunition to use against us.

Wednesday, June 27

It looks as if we will not be getting any help from the Democratic Assembly campaign committee. While this is hardly a surprise, the way it happened is hard to believe. The state party wanted us to take a poll. We would pay for the phone bank and supply the volunteers to interview four hundred people. They would supply the sample and the questions. We estimated that our share of the cost could be close to a thousand dollars. Then we discovered how little we were getting in return. The sample was a list of over four thousand registered voters with their addresses. Our volunteers would have to look up their phone numbers, after which we would have to choose a random four hundred people, train our volunteers, and conduct interviews of about twenty minutes, assuming that most people did not hang up before then (in which case we would have to disregard the interview and try someone else). People with unlisted numbers, people who had moved during the last year, and most students (a group that we hoped to mobilize) would be omitted.

The poll itself was their generic model with a few variations whose main goal seemed to be to explore every possible negative about Bill. One disturbing question attempted balance by saying a couple of good things about Bill, then asking "Some people say Bill Scheuerman is too liberal for the district. Do you agree?" Since at this stage of the campaign most people know little about the candidates, such questions would not only not help us, they would plant exactly the seed of doubt in four hundred voters' minds that our opponents would like to see grow. Unfortunately for us, the party has given the responsibility for campaigns they deem unimportant (like Bill's) to one of our former students who, despite a total lack of training about polls, thinks she knows more than we do. Bill had gotten nowhere with her so he turned to me.

Although I am not a pollster, I have written two books and numerous articles about how polls are used in campaigns so I am pretty knowledgeable about them. My critiques of some of the top pollsters have been well-received by many leading academics and practitioners. When I spoke to Ann, her response in essence was that the party has a certain way of doing things and would not modify it in any fashion, not even to consider questions that I would write. They would not do polls by committee. Of course, that is exactly what they were doing, the only difference being that they did not want us on their committee. Given the long odds of such a poll resulting in any significant financial aid, we have decided to go our own way. When Bill and I spoke about our decision, I told him to be sure he felt comfortable with it. He did but, having told Ann he would get back to her on Monday, has left himself a possible out. My conversation with Ann was so unpleasant that I know she will not be calling me again.

We decided to try to make all of this into a positive. We can use the money that is not going into the poll for advertising and printing literature. At most we would get a couple of thousand from the party so we have not lost much and if we can later demonstrate a close race, we may yet get something. Now Bill can emphasize that the state party is giving him nothing, so he will owe them nothing if elected. He can then ask his opponent how much money is coming from the Republican party and what will be expected in return. I asked Bill about the likelihood of getting money from the National Education Association (NEA). He thought we had a good chance although they have delayed their endorsement interviews until after the Republican primary selects a candidate. Tomorrow evening there will be a meeting of those active in the campaign, a core group that is now about twenty people. We will tell them of our problems with the state party to get some other views before we decide to tell Ann what to do with her poll. For the moment at least, we really are running an independent campaign.

Thursday, June 29

This evening we had a meeting of about fifteen of our leading campaign activists. If it served no other purpose, the meeting allowed us to get to know one another and, for many of those present, introduced the basic strategy. Bill introduced Jack Tyrie who ran the meeting. Jack did exactly what a good campaign manager should do, explaining that he is in charge of the day-to-day management of the campaign and that everyone should go through him with suggestions or complaints so as to free Bill to go out and campaign. Our emphasis on personal campaigning made this separation of responsibilities especially important since Bill will be making as many appearances as possible. His time and energy are our most important resources. Nevertheless, knowing Bill as well as I do, I am certain that, especially in a campaign as informally organized as ours, it will be hard to keep him out of most decisions. Jack told us that if we want to complain about anyone it should be him, never the candidate. He then updated the current situation. We have coordinators in most of the district's twenty-two towns. Although Bill will appear in all these towns, our strategy is to concentrate on the cities of Fulton and Oswego and the towns in the western part of the county. We need to organize on our own, expecting little or no help from the party. By now I was not surprised that no one had a good word to say about Lou Iorizzo as a party leader, not even a half-hearted defense such as, "at least he means well." No doubt we are being unfair. It is too much to expect a part-time party chair with few resources to provide all the help his candidates want.

Fortunately, when Jack told us that we have raised nearly three thousand dollars, no one saw Bill wince. In fact, we have raised less than half that. There were a number of new suggestions for fund-raisers. Carol Dwyer thought that she could get John Kennedy, Jr., who would surely attract a good crowd. Greg Auleta updated us on a possible concert. We also will arrange a pig roast if we can find a site. Several possible sites were discussed.

Jack gave us all a pep talk about how possible it would be to win the election despite the fact that he, like most local Democrats, has worked on so many losing campaigns. I amplified on this by providing an analysis of past election returns, showing where we could pick up votes. Jack then urged everyone to help recruit more people and started assigning specific responsibilities. People then brought up some local issues. Don Ritchie, a former student of ours who lives in Scriba and has relatives all over Fulton, brought up the renaming of Route 481. Local veterans organizations have pushed hard to change it to Veterans Memorial Highway but Ray Chesbro had so little influence that this cause had to be taken up by an Assemblyman from Syracuse. This issue could help Bill get some endorsements but he must be careful to avoid direct attacks on the lack of influence of the popular Chesbro.

Many people knew about specific events that Bill could attend. One of the most important was the farm bureau meeting at which both Bill and his opponent will be present. Since Nancy would moderate and, as far as we knew, Frances Sullivan was no expert on farm issues, this should help Bill pick up farm votes. We hope to get him in front of enough voters to overcome the inevitable attacks on him as a New York City college professor liberal, a tag the Republicans will try to pin on him once the formal campaign begins in September. Just as voters who saw Ronald Reagan in 1980 found it hard to believe that this nice man could possibly be a warmonger, we hope that most people who meet Bill will be too impressed by his energy and identification with the average person to find standard attacks on him credible.

After the meeting, a few of us stayed. I suggested that we try to use the two days before classes start at the college to have Bill give a few talks to students and register as many students as possible. Except for new students and those in academic difficulties who must change their schedules, most students have little to do those days. With the president of Student Association in our corner, we can sign up quite a few potential voters and perhaps even add some volunteers. Jack and I will also work on a short poll that some of our volunteers could take. While not the best way to conduct a poll, it will be within our budget and could provide some useful information about issues and voter familiarity with the candidates.

Tomorrow Bill will meet with Muriel Allerton, the Democratic mayor of Fulton. Muriel is a nice person who can be a great help to us. I estimate that we need about 13,000 to 14,000 votes to win if Yerdon runs as a third-party candidate, about 15,000 if he does not. Turnout in the city of Oswego should be about 6,500; Fulton about 4,500. If we can get close to 60 percent of the two-party vote in Oswego and 55 percent in Fulton, this will provide nearly half the votes necessary to win. However, Sullivan comes from Volney, a suburb of Fulton, so 55 percent in Fulton may be a bit optimistic. If so, those votes will have to be made up elsewhere. Muriel may also be able to help us add more volunteers and raise money. After meeting with Muriel, Bill will be interviewed by the main Oswego newspaper, the *Palladium-Times*.

Sunday, July 1

When I went to buy the Sunday paper this morning, I ran into a member of the History Department who, having been impressed with our fund-raising letter, asked if I would accept a contribution. His fifty-dollar check was a great start to the day. Bill thinks his newspaper interview went well, especially since the interviewers pretty much let him set the agenda. As a result, he was able to stress some of his big issues such as how to improve the state's budget process and consumer protection without having to field a single question on Republican issues such as capital punishment. I continue to be amazed and wonder how long our good fortune on the death penalty issue will keep up.

The big event of the day for everyone in the county was the parade. More than ten thousand people came from near and far to line the streets of the city of Oswego. Lou had told us that the party would put in Bill's name for a float but by now we knew enough to check on this early enough to put ourselves in. To no one's surprise, we discovered that nothing had been done but were able to get Bill's name in on time. We decorated John Wilson's truck

Bill with young supporters (including daughter Liesel on far left) at the 4th of July parade in Oswego.

in accord with the Fourth of July theme. Our best touch was to arrange for Bill's teenage daughter Liesel and a few of her friends to march in front of the truck, carrying signs and wearing "Scheuerman for Assembly" T-shirts. Bill and Louise marched between the girls, waving to the crowd. Gene and Suzanne Basualdo, Bill's next-door neighbors, and I followed along, distributing Bill's cards to as many of the spectators as possible. Amazingly, this all worked as planned. Bill occasionally walked into the crowd to shake hands and chat briefly. Our early training period has whipped him into shape, giving him an ease and efficiency with people that will be a major asset. We now joke that his best constituency is all the older women that he has kissed along the campaign trail.

Fran Sullivan also had a place in the parade but she stayed in her car and waved, stepping out only to introduce herself to Bill. This was a friendly gesture on her part and the two had a short but pleasant chat. We were able to pick up a piece of her literature that is much fancier than ours but the basic information it contained does not worry us. It appears likely that she will have a tough primary against Mike Yerdon who was also at the parade. We will know for certain when petitions are turned in about two weeks from now.

The one minus for the day was that, despite all the broadcast coverage of the parade in the media, no mention was made of the candidates for assembly. The only mention of political candidates by the media was Jerry Herrington's accidently stepping in horse excrement but recovering by making a joke out of it. Critics have often argued that media coverage of elections concentrates not on substantive issues but on the horse-race aspects but I doubt that they had this in mind.

Tuesday, July 3

Today's meeting with the vegetable growers went exceptionally well. Bill did his homework and it showed. For example, he argued that the only long-term solution to the problems of farmers is research into new products and new techniques. Surely we can use the resources of SUNY yet our short-sighted budget has done the opposite. For the past two years there has been a program to develop an onion that would be bacteria-resistant. Because it would not need pesticides, such an onion would be profitable for farmers while satisfying complaints of environmentalists. Yet this year's budget cut the $50,000 program out. As a union officer, Bill has fought for such programs but could do far more as an assemblyman. These overwhelmingly Republican farmers were disillusioned with the status quo. Although they will take some of this out on the governor, a number of them indicated that they could also wind up supporting Bill. If he can get even 40 percent of their vote together with big majorities in the cities, we could win.

On the negative side, the county committee has done it again. When Bill and Jack went to apply for a booth at the county fair, they were told that the deadline has passed. No problem, they thought, we can use the Democratic party's booth. Unfortunately, even though the fair organizers sent the party an application, it was never filled out. This Democratic inaction has caused us to worry about our petitions. After calling several of those who should have been circulating them, we found some disturbing news. Although the party gave them out, very few people have even begun gathering signatures. As a result we have to get together on Saturday to circulate some on our own or we may fail to get on the ballot. Having to do so is more than a minor inconvenience since we want to have a second ballot line for those people allergic to the Democratic lever. New York regulations require that independent petitions be circulated only by people who have neither signed nor circulated party petitions. They also require three times as many signatures as party petitions, one of many mechanisms designed to protect the major parties. If our volunteers have to circulate our party petitions, it will make it that much harder to get our independent line.

Needless to say, there is much dissatisfaction with Lou's party leadership. A party that may not even be able to get its own candidates on the ballot is awfully feeble even in the context of the current state of political parties. Because Lou's term does not end until September 1991, not much can be done now without a divisive internal fight that would only hurt us. But if Bill wins, there will be big changes in the county party.

Thursday, July 5

The weekly farmers' markets in Oswego on Thursday evenings and Fulton on Saturday mornings have become regular campaign stops. Oswego's is by far the busier of the two. By now, Bill has become very adept at introducing himself to strangers. At this early stage he is simply saying that he is not yet asking for their vote, only that they listen to his message in the next few months and decide which candidate to vote for on the merits. Most people listen politely and sympathetically with virtually no one running away or arguing. A few people stay for more than a few moments, either to ask a question or just to chat about a subject of interest to them. Sometimes this is quite productive as it was with a woman who asked Bill his position on abortion. After he told her he opposed government intervention in the woman's decision, he paused, not knowing whether to be hopeful or apprehensive. He was pleased and relieved to learn that she had left the Republican Party because it had taken the opposite position. She would be glad to vote for him.

One young couple with a baby in tow was pleased to learn about Bill's union position since the husband was a union pipefitter apprehensive about the local economy. We even were able to register a few potential voters. If we are lucky we got perhaps ten votes out of all of this. But we added considerably to Bill's name recognition, having spoken to a couple of hundred people and handed them cards. We are trying to pick our spots and add up enough small gains to make progress almost imperceptibly. We have heard that the Republicans are beginning to take notice, especially worrying about Bill's efforts in farm areas. On the one hand, this is a good sign. On the other, we have been hoping to get a good start by not being noticed for a few months. The Republicans will be bringing out the heavy artillery a little earlier than we wanted so we had better keep moving.

Saturday, July 7

Even though we heard that a number of the party committee people were circulating our petitions with about three hundred of the necessary five hundred signatures collected, we decided that a few of us should go out to collect some signatures for insurance. While we were out we took petitions for several other candidates (including Jack's for state committee) but deliberately decided not to circulate the judicial petitions that are primarily the party's responsibility. As a result, John Wilson and I had to do some quick thinking when we ran into John and Charlotte Sullivan, who signed our petitions but asked where the judicial ones were. We replied that we understood that both Bill and the judicial candidates had enough signatures. Our goal was merely to show how widespread Bill's support was by turning in petitions covering as many parts of the district and wards of the city as possible. Let's hope that worked.

Otherwise, our rounds of the city went very well. Quite a few people had seen Bill either at the parade or the farmers' market. Nearly all of them had a favorable impression. There was only one specific issue question, by a woman who was delighted to hear that Bill was pro-choice. John dropped into two fraternity houses that had students still living there during the summer. They expressed interest in the campaign (despite a few hangovers in one frat house) and told us that their fraternities would be glad to help register students when the semester started. Although we should not have had to circulate the petitions ourselves, the morning produced some successful campaigning, with several long conversations describing just who Bill was. As for the candidate, he had the usual busy weekend, including campaigning in Fulton both Saturday and Sunday as well as in Hastings and Phoenix today. Then he would be off to his job in Albany on Sunday night. He could be one of the few people for whom commuting to assembly sessions would mean less travel.

Tuesday, July 10

Today Jack and I got together to work on a poll for the campaign. Before we started, Jack told me that there appeared to be enough petition signatures to get all the candidates on the ballot except for Jerry Herrington. All that surprised us was that this was the only screw-up. It means that poor Jerry will have to get some of his supporters together to scramble for the additional hundred or so signatures (plus some extras in case of a challenge) or his run for sheriff will evaporate. Fortunately, his was one of the petitions we took out on Saturday so we can provide a little help.

As for the poll, I had some ideas for making it easier to do and more useful for us than the one the state party tried to force on us. Instead of using last year's list of registered voters, which our petition drive indicated contained many obsolete addresses and which would force us to look up all the phone numbers, I suggested we use random digit dialing. When I explained how this would work, Jack liked the idea. However, it would increase the number of people we interview who may not vote. For us, the trade-off is well worth it and we could increase our sample and include a filter question if necessary. Our main problem is developing a short questionnaire that will provide us with the most useful information. I had written a few possible questions and had some general ideas. We decided to ask about the following:

1. How voters rate Cuomo's performance as governor. This will help us decide whether we want to emphasize the areas where Bill agrees with him or those where he does not. We also need to know just how much we want to ride his coattails. Having come across a great deal of anti-Cuomo sentiment in our campaigning so far, we need some objective data.
2. What the public thinks about the three assembly candidates. It is too early for such trial heats to be predictive of anything but they will let us know something about name recognition and the strength of voters' party affiliation.
3. Issues. Here we will ask what voters consider the most important problem facing the legislature as well as specific questions about abortion, the budget, Bill's scanner critique, cable television regulation, and how people feel about spending on several government programs. We see no need to ask about capital punishment since we know an overwhelming majority favors it. The abortion question will give respondents three

choices—the right to life position, Sullivan's position allowing abortions for rape and incest, and Bill's pro-choice position. We will describe each of these, of course, not labeling them with any identifications.
4. What characteristics voters are looking for in a candidate for assembly. Jack likes my question asking voters to choose one from among several choices: experience in elective office, fighting vigorously for the district, belonging to my political party, having conservative ideas, and being born in the district.
5. Demographic information. This includes party identification, age, sex, residence, etc.

I will instruct the volunteers who will be calling as well as make up the script for them to read from. However, I will be going on a ten-day vacation starting next week so I told Jack how to instruct callers in case the poll is taken while I am away. I was well prepared for our meeting, bringing a typed list of possible questions with me. We were able to work quickly. I will check my final version with Bill to see if he wants to add anything. Then we will be ready to go once we rent a phone bank and find a good date for our volunteers.

Thursday, July 12

We turned our petitions in today. With more than twice the necessary five hundred signatures, we were safe from challenge. Jerry Herrington got his in also but the big story was that Margaret Pavel has withdrawn her candidacy. Apparently she had been promised all sorts of help by both the state and local parties, virtually none of which (surprise) was delivered. Lou apparently hopes to induce someone to run, using some tricky mechanism for getting on the ballot. We heard that Jim Soluri is a possibility. Jim is articulate, intelligent, and well regarded. This would ordinarily make him an excellent candidate, but he is also a member of the college's Music Department. The lack of balance of a ticket with two male college professors as the legislative candidates would damage its electoral appeal considerably. With Bill likely to be running against a woman, having a woman running not only alongside him but also for the more prestigious office would have deflected a great deal of potential opposition. Although we both know Jim pretty well, neither of us had discussed this with him, so we had no idea whether he has any interest in running a race that at this point looks totally hopeless.

Better news is the fact that both Yerdon and Sullivan turned in petitions, guaranteeing a primary. Our next job is to get Bill a second line on the ballot by circulating independent petitions, which we can do starting today. Since tonight is the Oswego farmers' market, we began work right away. Bill and John Wilson went off to shake hands while Louise, Gene and Suzanne Basualdo, and I set up a table to hand out literature and get signatures. During the hour and a half that I was there, we got about sixty. I think this is a good start. Independent petitions require 1,500 signatures compared to the five hundred for the major parties (fairly typical legal discrimination). So we have a lot of work to do, but a reasonable amount of time to do it in if our volunteers come through. We even got a signature of a registered Right to Life Party voter who, fortunately for us, never asked about Bill's position on abortion. Of course, had she asked, we would have told her and lost her signature. No doubt she will find it out before election day and vote against Bill unless we are lucky enough for her not to vote in this race. This could happen. The state Republican Party and its gubernatorial candidate are pro-choice while Frances Sullivan would allow some abortions even though she is not pro-choice.

Sunday, July 15

Studying farm issues again paid off for Bill in today's first joint appearance of the three candidates before the Farm Bureau. Neither of his opponents seems to have done any such preparation, speaking in clichéd generalities instead. Sullivan did not even arrive on time. Yerdon will get significant support from farmers simply by coming from a rural area and having a good-old-boy manner. Nevertheless, the contrast between the two Republicans and Bill was so striking that after the discussion most of those present went directly to him for congratulations.

The debate was not limited to farm issues. Bill had to answer some tough questions on capital punishment and abortion. He laid out his pro-choice stance in light of his own family and religious beliefs. Afterward, I suggested that he emphasize more that he and Louise chose to have three children and are glad they did, an idea he liked. We know Bill will lose some votes because of abortion

56

but believe that he will gain far more. As for capital punishment, he told those present that he would vote for it but that the legislature and both Cuomo and his predecessor had been playing political games. Year after year, the legislature passes a death penalty bill, the governor vetoes it, the veto is sustained, and nothing constructive results. Bill would not only vote for capital punishment; if another veto was sustained, he would work for life imprisonment without parole so that something could be done now. As I suggested, he stressed his experience as a parole officer and what it had taught him about crime. In the long run the only solution was to attack the conditions that caused crime. But we also needed to take measures for the present. It was time to stop playing political games and start to get something done. Overall, Bill did so well that Sullivan made an excuse and left early. This more than made up for the fact that the legislature passed the bill renaming Route 481 Veterans Memorial Highway, taking away from us a useful secondary issue.

Tomorrow, we will get to a more routine task. We drafted a letter to be sent to all those who signed Bill's Democratic petitions, asking for support. In our low-tech campaign, we will address and stuff the envelopes by hand. I will also give Jack the final version of our poll. Then I will be away for a vacation.

Monday, July 30

While I was away, Lou's selection of a state senate candidate created quite a stir. He chose Mary Kay Dowd, a former chair of the local Conservative Party. She had resigned that position several years ago not out of disagreement with the party on issues, but because of her indictment for forging petition signatures. Subsequently she defended herself with the argument that she had never been convicted on those felony charges. This was only true because the eventual plea bargain resulted in a misdemeanor conviction. Lou, who has consistently told us that the party has no money to contribute, managed to find a local auto dealer to lend a car for her campaign. Needless to say, the reaction among party activists to her selection has been negative. Some party committee members even wanted to remove Lou, but he has weathered that storm for now. Despite many abstentions, the county committee voted to endorse her. Many local party activists have told Bill that they would not support him if he even appeared on the same platform with her. The other party chairs in the senate district have evaded the issue by saying that her candidacy is Lou's work and they will support it. This has created a problem for us. We do not wish to divide the party further by attacking one of our own candidates. If Bill is asked about her candidacy, the best response we have been able to devise is that, since he has asked the voters in his race to vote for the person best qualified without regard to party, he trusts those same voters to make the right choice in other races as well. Because Bill has stressed his independence from the party at every opportunity, this rather tepid response may suffice.

Over the weekend, Bill's booth at Harborfest, the city of Oswego's biggest event of the year, was successful in getting about six hundred of the necessary 1,500 signatures on our petition for an independent line. With two weeks left, we should be able to make it with enough extra signatures to withstand any challenges. Both Yerdon and Sullivan had booths as well but stayed behind them waiting for people to come to them rather than going out in search of voters. Bill has become so expert at mingling that we contacted far more people than they did. We are going to need to do so because the Republican Party has already started buying newspaper ads for Frances Sullivan.

Friday, August 3

Bill's office in Albany was closed this week so he has been resting at home. We spent the morning playing golf, mixing in some discussion of the campaign. Money remains our biggest problem. John Sullivan's fund-raising letter has so far resulted in very little return, probably because he asked the same group for money shortly before turning the list over to us. The best sources of funds so far have been SUNY people and some local politicians and lawyers Bill has worked with. If we can hang on until after the Republican primary, we should get a few thousand from some local unions and a similar amount from statewide teachers' unions. Meanwhile, we have to work with the little we have. Bill was slightly discouraged by this, but it did not take much effort to get him in a better mood. I told him that a couple of people we know from graduate school have offered to contribute so he will remind them with a letter. We have been able to afford bumper stickers to increase our visibility. In addition, Gene Basualdo has made up more than fifty mini-billboards that have been placed on people's front lawns.

In fact, Gene has been one of the campaign's most valuable resources. At first, we kidded each other when he said he could deliver the Hispanic vote, but we have stopped laughing. Apparently, during the last couple of years, there has been a significant migration of Spanish-speaking people into the county. But, because they have tended to keep to themselves, it has not been visible to most. Gene has been able to reach many of them at church gatherings and is confident that his voter registration drives will mobilize at least a few hundred votes. In addition, some migrant workers have resided here long enough to be eligible to vote by absentee ballot. Oswego is a very conservative county, so we have had to overcome some resistance to Gene's efforts. For example, the Board of Elections has no Spanish language materials, nor would it make any effort to get them. Gene, however, has been so persistent that it appears no obstacles will even slow him down.

Bill continues to do well with farmers because of his knowledge of farm issues coupled with his declaration of independence from the state party. He backs this up by pointing out that they are giving him no money at all. Quite a few of the vegetable growers have indicated that they will vote for him. If Sullivan is nominated, we may even get some financial help. Even though her ads have stressed that she is a native of the county and grew up on a dairy farm, she knows little about farm issues and the farmers who have seen her know it. Bill has also met several times with Nancy Larraine Hoffman, the only Democratic senator from this area. Nancy has survived in a Republican district largely because of her excellent record of constituent service. Farmers have been especially supportive of her. She has offered to help Bill in any way she can. We took a few pictures of the two together that, when the finances permit, we will use in newspaper ads.

Sunday, August 12

This was a very busy weekend for Bill. In the interests of equity, the organizers of the County Fair ignored their deadline and gave us a booth. Since the Fulton River Fest occured simultaneously with the County Fair, Bill made even more appearances than usual. Our primary goal was to get signatures for independent petitions, which are due next week. Although we have already gathered about five hundred more than the required 1,500, our research indicates that some who claim to be registered voters when signing are not. New

York's law is so technical that anyone who does not sign exactly as on his or her official registration (leaving out a middle initial, for example) is vulnerable to a challenge. We are not yet sure just how many questionable signatures there are, but to withstand a possible challenge we need to get a few hundred more as insurance.

It is time to work out some of our strategy for the fall. Jack wants to do a mass mailing but Bill and I disagree. Such a mailing would cost us several thousand dollars. With our limited budget, this is not an efficient way to reach voters. A single mailing would have limited impact. This is one time that more efficient technology would be less costly for us than old-fashioned methods. Because media is so cheap in Oswego county, we could spend less for several rounds of radio and newspaper ads that will reach most potential voters not once but several times. With Bill so little known right now, the repetition of his message and qualifications will have far more impact than a single mailing that most recipients are likely to throw away unread. A limited budget like ours can only afford targeted mailings. One obvious idea is to get union membership lists and send them a letter emphasizing Bill's union background and any labor endorsements he can get.

I will be meeting with Paul Austin, the president of the college's Student Association, on Wednesday. Paul has been very enthusiastic about the campaign. He has already organized a voter registration drive for students and wants to do more, so we will work out a role for him. Paul is a bright guy with a real interest in politics so he could be very helpful. Students will be coming back to campus in about two weeks and we will need to recruit as many as we can to help us out in the campaign.

Thursday, August 16

After a few setbacks, things are looking up. Paul Austin failed to appear for our meeting and left no message of any kind. By now I should know that students are often less reliable in following up their enthusiasms but I never fail to be disappointed when it does happen. Eventually, I will see Paul or, if not, other students who will do something for us. Bill was even more disappointed to learn that the local painters' union, with great fanfare, endorsed Fran Sullivan without even speaking to him or anyone in our campaign to learn our issue positions. Clearly, local friendships often mean more than substance. We learned that this endorsement was arranged in April, before there even was a Democratic candidate, so there was little we could do.

Fortunately, some positives more than outweighed these negatives. The New York State United Teachers, our parent union, endorsed Bill. Ordinarily, being endorsed by your own union would not be very big news but NYSUT has a policy of not making endorsements for open seat races. With a lot of help from UUP, especially President Tim Reilly and past President Nuala Drescher, we got them to make an exception. This will mean much needed funds. We expect a few thousand dollars with which we can purchase at least a minimal amount of media. Coupled with this were endorsements from two of the most important local unions in Fulton, the chocolate workers at the Nestle plant and the machinists at the Miller Brewery. Bill and I wrote press releases playing up these endorsements. We also included some basic statements on issues of interest to workers such as tax equity and job security. We are holding back the NYSUT endorsement not only to make it a separate news event but also because it is not yet official. We have to wait until they make their own announcement. Because we have promises of more endorsements, our hope is to generate a steady flow of news stories to keep Bill quietly but favorably in the news while the Republicans battle it out in their primary.

These endorsements will also be bringing in more money, probably after next month's primary. With the assurance of adequate funds for advertising, Jack, Rand Bishop (a member of the English Department who has been working for us), Andy Hillman (one of the few party committee people who has been working hard), and I plan to get together Monday to devise an advertising plan. In the few days after that we will write the text of our first ads, one for radio and one for newspapers. Radio is by far the most cost effective. We can buy ten one-minute spots on Oswego's leading commercial station for only seventy dollars (that's total cost, not cost per ad!) compared to one hundred dollars for a quarter page in the *Oswego Palladium Times.* To cover the district, we need to devise a buying plan to include the local weeklies and the smaller radio stations.

Although it took some prodding on our part, the party has provided some important help, paying for the printing of stationery and 20,000 brochures. It has been easy to snipe at Lou but this time he has done the job. The brochure contains pictures and biographies of Bill and Jerry Herrington but, because it was printed between Meg Pavel's withdrawal and Mary Kay Dowd's candidacy, makes no mention of a Senate candidate. This was very fortuitous timing for us but we are not sure that Lou is convinced it was entirely an accident. We have also scheduled a fund-raiser in Fulton—a pig roast on August 25. Bill has been making his usual round of appearances, including a parade tonight. We are also making a last-minute push for a few hundred more petition signatures to ensure a second ballot line.

Monday, August 20

Today Jack, Rand, Andy, and I got together to plan our advertising. Because of its low cost, radio will be our primary medium with some newspaper ads to supplement it. Starting around Labor Day we will run two weeks of radio ads to introduce Bill; a serious one about why he is running, alternating with a humorous one about pronouncing his last name. After that we will introduce a new theme every couple of weeks. We worked out a schedule to introduce such issues as a pledge to oppose any legislative salary increases, the budget, consumer issues, farm issues (to be used primarily on the country music station), jobs, children's issues—education and day care, for example—and a few others. We will try to finish with an endorsement ad followed by an ad stressing the grass-roots nature of Bill's campaign while he explains what he has done and what he has learned during the campaign. Overall, our theme emphasizes that Bill is a candidate who opposes politics as usual. The issues will be presented to demonstrate just how he will do so if elected. The first newspaper ad will be a simple biographical one with information similar to our brochure. We are all in agreement with these ideas. We will present them to Bill on Thursday. Our petitions, with more than 2,500 signatures, are also ready to be turned in tomorrow.

Wednesday, August 22

Our first major crisis was a real beauty. Chuck Ely, the county Republican party chair, called Lou with a serious threat. He claimed that he has evidence of irregularities in our independent petitions and will press criminal charges if Bill does not withdraw them in three days, thus surrendering the extra ballot line. Apparently, he had people follow the petition gatherers at Harborfest and other large events and they saw different people getting signatures for a single petition. Since only one person signed each petition sheet of twenty signatures, petition gatherers allegedly signed sworn statements that they had witnessed signatures when in fact they had not. Bill was very worried and called a meeting to see what had happened. I feel that we have no choice but to see what evidence they have and ride it out. When similar incidents occurred in the past, the Republicans usually tried to press charges even after petitions were withdrawn. Thus, the withdrawal would not protect anyone. But it would be a political disaster because it would appear to admit guilt. Furthermore, this is not a very serious scandal, amounting to little more than a charge of carelessness by inexperienced volunteers. Past criminal charges involved the forging of signatures. In this case, all the signatures were true ones that had been witnessed; the only possible error was that the wrong witness had signed the petition. We could charge Republican dirty tricks and, should there be a trial, call Ely and all those whose job was to follow us. Thus, such charges could backfire against those who made them. After all, bringing such minor charges is a very poor way to spend the taxpayers' money.

We got some legal advice as well, both from John Sullivan, who is an attorney, and a party lawyer in Albany who specializes in election law. In essence, they said that any criminal charges would be unlikely to get very far since there was no evidence of criminal intent. Basically, we would be claiming incompetence by a few volunteers. The only serious risk would be if such errors were so widespread that they implied more deliberate action. At our meeting, we tried to reconstruct the events that had occurred. There seemed very little evidence of mistakes. In some cases, a husband and wife were working together so both saw each signature. If so, it really did not matter which of them signed the witness statement. Everyone agreed to wait and see what evidence the Republicans had and try our best to ride out the storm. We tried to make sure that each person knew the risks should criminal charges be brought. Fortunately, I was not in jeopardy, having been very careful to circulate my petitions alone, sign all of them, and not sign any circulated by anyone else. But those at risk were willing to shoulder any bad publicity that could come their way. The campaign itself would schedule a fund-raiser to take care of any legal expenses if necessary. We asked Bill if he had circulated any petitions. He had, but with only two signatures he was not in any danger. Everyone was relieved by this, not only because it would avoid the worst publicity, but also because false witnessing by a candidate is a felony compared to a misdemeanor for his or her aides.

This carelessness will definitely hurt us. Even if we can handle bad publicity, scarce resources will have to be diverted to our defense. There should have been a thorough orientation for people who had never circulated petitions before. Of course, this lesson will do us no good if we lose the election.

Thursday, August 23

Bill dropped in unannounced. He was really a nervous wreck. Because he is a worrier with all the associated signs — a mild ulcer, restlessness — I thought it was simply the anxiety of waiting to see just how bad the petition problem would turn out to be, but he had come with even more bad news. While looking at our copies of the petitions, he discovered that he had circulated another petition but must have forgotten to sign it and left it at home in a pile of Louise's petitions. In the confusion, she signed it along with hers. One of the signatures he had gotten was that of a Republican alderman whom Ely will be sure to call. What now? My first impulse was to ask him how he could have been so stupid. But he was so distressed that no friend would do this. I tried as best as I could be reassuring. Let's wait and see what happens, I told him. A lot of politics is appearance so you have to show a confident front. He called John Sullivan, who was very nice about giving him time and advice and was as reassuring as possible. He helped calm Bill a little. For now, I said, go home and mow the lawn.

Saturday, August 25

Even though I know that campaigns are full of ups and downs, I am amazed at how sharp these are. After consulting with numerous attorneys and thinking matters over, we have concluded that we overreacted to Ely's petition threat. A few minor mistakes made by people with little political experience do not add up to a criminal offense. Since the signatures are legitimate, having the wrong witness sign at the bottom of the form gained nothing for the campaign and could cost us the entire twenty signatures on the sheet. The county district attorney, although nominally a Republican, is a fair-minded prosecutor who is unlikely to take such charges to a grand jury. At worst, the Republicans will challenge our petitions, a very normal occurrence. Unfortunately, Bill will be at the AFL-CIO convention working for their endorsement this week so we wrote a possible press release and discussed what we would do should anything occur while he is out of town.

But while we were working this out, good things were happening. Bill previously contacted several public sector unions in the hope of getting endorsements. Yesterday, the corrections officers' union told him that no one else in the district has even asked them and, having worked with Bill on working environment issues in the past, they are inclined to endorse him depending upon his position on a few issues of importance to them. What is his position on capital punishment? When he told them that he would vote for it, then added that he had been a parole officer, they were impressed. After a few more questions, they agreed to endorse him. This is a big success that we plan to publicize as widely as possible because it will prevent the Republicans from attacking Bill as being soft on crime.

The pig roast exceeded our hopes. Instead of the seventy-five or so people we expected, two hundred bought tickets at either seven dollars and fifty cents or ten dollars each, resulting in a profit of around $1,500. When Jim McMahon ran, he held a fund-raiser in Fulton that attracted only twenty contributors. We have also learned something about merchandising, selling T-shirts and running a raffle during the event. With small contributions coming in and some union money on the way, we expect to have an adequate budget for our needs. We might even be able to put aside a few thousand dollars for a last-week advertising campaign. If we can get Jack to move a little faster in putting together a final script and reserving studio times, we will be on radio in a week or two.

At the pig roast, Bill made a well-received short speech emphasizing his major campaign themes. Although reaction was enthusiastic, I suggested some improvements. Unfortunately, there have been few occasions during the campaign for set speeches by Bill. He is a far better speaker than either Yerdon or Sullivan, so it is just a question of getting him a bit of practice. Even though set speeches generally do not mean much in this district, every little bit will help.

Tuesday, August 28

Today the petition story broke. Marc Heller of the *Palladium Times* called Jack, having heard the charges from his editor. The editor apparently learned of them from the attorney who filed the challenges to our petition, Kevin Caraccioli, rather than from Ely. Jack handled the issue very well, letting Marc know about Ely's threats, suggesting that the Republicans were utilizing desperate tactics to try to intimidate us, stressing our large number of signatures, stressing the volunteer nature of our campaign, and correcting the impression that had been given to Marc that these charges were felonies. Jack and I agreed that rather than immediately issuing our press release, we should wait to see what came out in this afternoon's paper. If the charges were treated as being silly, we did not want to overreact with a slashing counterattack. Bill eventually called each of us. Probably feeling frustrated by not being on the scene, he wanted to issue the release right away but we talked him out of it, suggesting that we would talk to him later in the day.

The results exceeded our expectations. Under the headline, "Attorney will drop challenges," the front-page story indicated that Caraccioli would not file charges against us, and that he was withdrawing his challenges to our petitions, stating, "We've come up with very little in the way of invalid petitions." Even better was Ely's absurd denial that the Republicans were behind the challenge. When asked about his threatening call to Lou, he refused to either confirm or deny it, lamely replying that any conversations he had were a private matter. He ended by saying that he had no intention of filing criminal charges and that the challenge was not intended to eliminate anyone from the campaign. Since he claimed that the Republicans were not behind the challenge, a reader might wonder how he knew their purpose. In any case, round one went to us.

Impatient, Bill called me to discuss events. He wanted to follow up by demanding an apology from Ely, something I argued against. Our goal is to conduct a campaign on candidate qualifications and issues. Fighting it out with Ely would make Bill look like just another politician jockeying for position. Let's take our small victory and move on to the campaign we want to wage. Bill reluctantly agreed. I put this reluctance down to his being out of town and feeling powerless. Once he gets back on the campaign trail, he will realize we did the right thing.

Wednesday, August 29

Jack and I met for about an hour to go over some press releases and a radio ad that Rand Bishop wrote. They include my idea of

66

a pledge not only to oppose a salary increase for state legislators but also to refuse to accept one should it be passed during Bill's first term. In addition, Bill supports a proposal to cut off the salaries of both the governor and the state legislature should it again fail to pass a budget on time. Rand's ads are usually good but he lacks a sense of the nuance necessary to get across our main points without including other distracting information. With some editing on our part, we have a good script for our second week of ads. Bill already taped our first set, which will be running next week. He also visited the offices of a couple of the local weekly shoppers, run by Republican supporters, and pressed them to promise to cover at least some of his activities. He claims that he was so obnoxious that they had to agree although I am sure he was obnoxious in a very polite manner.

Saturday, September 1

Bill has been complaining that Jack has been tardy in getting things done. I had put this down to impatience on Bill's part as Jack always seems on top of things when I speak to him. But it now seems that Bill was right. Jack has been having some family problems. Although he said that they would not interfere with his work, Bill is not so sure. Since Jack has a lot to contribute, I suggested that we find some ways to give him assistance. I have already arranged to get a student intern to help. We can give her a key to party headquarters and delegate some of Jack's work to her—distributing press releases to the media, scheduling meetings, writing thank-you notes to contributors, etc. Karen Madden is a capable and dependable person who worked in a state senator's office during the summer. Once she gets the hang of what we are doing, we expect to be able to assign more serious responsibilities to her. I will take over the writing of as many press releases as possible. This will make life easier for both Jack and Bill because I am better than Jack at writing in Bill's style. The result will likely be to reduce the changes that Bill will have to make from the draft to the final version. John Wilson, who has been tireless, will also be given more responsibility to speak for the campaign. I hope that our new arrangement will work out. Because of Jack's enthusiasm about the campaign, I do not think it would be fair to replace him unless he wants out. In a campaign like ours, the candidate is too involved with all the details, magnifying small problems into major crises.

Sunday, September 2

Bill has appeared at Fireman's Field Days in Redfield, a rural Republican stronghold. Even though we had not planned to give that area much attention, a few appearances could help us pick up a small number of votes and also show that we are not writing off any of the towns. More importantly, this is Yerdon's hometown. Should he lose the primary, we hope to convince as many of his supporters as possible to vote for Bill as their second choice, remembering that Yerdon used to be a Democrat. In fact, his brother is still the town's most prominent Democrat. Bill, with the skillful accompaniment of John Wilson, succeeded better than we had hoped. As always, most of those who met him came away with a positive impression. John Yerdon, who is of course supporting brother Mike, told the crowd that if his brother were not a candidate, he would have supported Bill. There are probably only a couple of hundred voters in Redfield, but when Mike Yerdon ran as a Democrat in 1980 he won 77 percent, an extraordinary percentage in a Republican area. If we could pick up some votes in Redfield and other nearby towns they would be coming out of the Republican base.

This evening I had a meeting with Bill, Jack, Rand, and Jim Clemens to go over advertising strategy. Jim volunteered for the campaign early in the summer and has been one of our best people. He has always wanted to work for Democratic candidates but has never been given the chance. We are glad to have been the first to listen to him. He is a tireless worker. Given the nature of our campaign organization, this quality is all it really takes to rise to the upper levels. I wrote a press release to go with our salary ads. It headlined a new proposal by Bill for a four-year salary freeze for the state legislature together with the other promises included in Rand's radio ad. We agreed to distribute it without changes, confirming my view that having me write these will reduce other people's need to edit. We expect coverage of this in the local papers to coordinate with our advertising theme. Bill has already been interviewed by the local radio station. It will play a sound bite of him discussing one of these proposals. Bill will soon tape the ad to run the week after next. We then worked on our ad schedule for the rest of the campaign, with ads on what we believe to be the major concerns of voters—consumer issues, education, the environment, jobs and the economy, farm issues, and crime, as well as a wrap-up ad at the end.

BILL SCHEUERMAN FOR STATE ASSEMBLY

★*Elected Town Supervisor - Minetto*

★*Elected Town Justice - Minetto*

★*Elected Vice President United University Professions, the nation's largest higher education union (20,000+ members)*

★*Member Oswego County Labor Council*

★*Chief Negotiator, $2 billion state wide contract*

★*Member, New York State Assembly Labor Committee, Interagency Task Force on Asbestos*

★*Founder, Coalition of Town Supervisors Against the Sterling Toxic Waste Dump*

★*Professor, Political Science - SUNY at Oswego*

★*Parole Officer, New York State Division of Parole*

★*Locomotive Engineer*

Vote November 6th for Bill Scheuerman
... The Common Sense Candidate ...

Inside copy of promotional brochure.

I will write the press release for our next theme, consumer issues, and Rand and Jack will work on the ads after reading my release. I plan to stress two subjects: the extension of the state's supermarket unit pricing law (the large chains using scanners oppose this, but it would be good for consumers), and the soaring cost of cable TV since deregulation. I will try to put it in the larger national context of consumer ripoffs from the S&L bailout to the recent surge in gasoline prices.

For at least the past fifteen years, the way to win an election has been to establish your candidate's themes. These themes, a mixture of the candidate's personality and background, style, and views on the issues, must be communicated clearly to voters. In our case, we are seeking to show that Bill runs counter to the public's perception of politicians, that he really does care about the average voter. We cannot do this simply by saying so. We have to provide evidence to back it up. Bill is our best asset. When people meet him, they quickly see that he cares about them, that he is a fighter, and that his positions on issues are in accord with his themes. Without television, however, and with a Republican advantage among party identifiers and in money, getting our message to voters will be a difficult task.

From my point of view, it is also important that Bill try to become better known without trying to make himself into someone other than himself. Despite the conservative nature of this district we cannot turn Bill into a conservative nor do we want to. As a matter of principle, it is important that Bill stick to his convictions. So far we have had to make only one compromise, although admittedly it is a big one: capital punishment. Part of my role is to act as the candidate's second conscience, prodding him about his essence whenever he is tempted to say something he does not believe. But back to our meeting.

We then went over our schedule of events for the near future. Rand is working on a run by Bill and others (definitely not including me!) from the center of the city of Oswego to the college campus, ending in a short speech by Bill and a voter registration drive. Since voters have to register at least thirty days before the election, we have to get going on this as well as our campus voter registration drive. I managed to speak to Paul Austin who has promised to arrange one or two candidates' forums on campus. Without any evidence, I think he will come through this time.

We also were able to print up a few thousand copies of a new brochure with pictures of Bill and his family, a list of some of the relevant positions he has held, and very brief statements (one or two sentences each) on half a dozen major issues. Emphasizing Bill's independence (and bowing to the overwhelming Republican registration advantage), the pamphlet does not contain the word "Democrat," instead describing Bill as "The Common Sense Candidate," the name of our independent line. Because early reaction to the brochure has been good, our next version will keep it basically the same with the addition of a list of some of the groups that have endorsed Bill. We also discussed whether to take my suggested poll or not. I now believe that there is no real need to do so but we decided to wait until after the Republican primary before making a final decision.

If nothing else, we have learned enough about one another and how to run a meeting that we were able to conduct this one relatively briefly and efficiently. In the peaks and valleys of the campaign we were, for the moment at least, in a period of optimism.

Saturday, September 8

It has been a quiet week as we await the results of Tuesday's Republican primary. Now that classes have begun, I have been working to get more students involved in the campaign. Karen has worked out a set of duties and a tentative schedule with Jack. Former Student Association Vice-President Emilio Dorcely will also be an intern, concentrating at first on getting students registered. Paul Austin will let me know of some dates for a possible candidate forum on campus, something we would like to arrange as soon after the primary as possible. The Young Democrats, an organization that has been dormant for some time, is now being revived. I spoke to one of the revivers who was very interested in having Bill talk before the group. He promised to call Bill to make arrangements.

Finally, I spoke to the editor of the campus newspaper about interviewing Bill. Not surprisingly, she liked the idea and will have the news editor call me to work out the details. Because we need a lot of student votes to win, we have to start early. Voter registration closes about a month before the election. John Wilson spoke to several fraternity and sorority leaders (because of my strong emphasis on academics, I have not always gotten along well with these groups) about helping out. As a result of these conversations, he is confident that they will do something. Jack fears that, if students do turn out, many will vote Republican as has sometimes been the case in the past. But I believe that if we can expose them to Bill, he will get an overwhelming majority of their votes.

Newspaper coverage is slowly coming along. The main daily paper, the *Palladium Times,* is based in the city of Oswego but covers the whole district. With Marc Heller covering the campaign for them, we are confident of fair coverage. Most of the other papers are localized weeklies and shoppers, many of which are owned by prominent Republicans. The most politically oriented are the *Oswego Valley News* and *Eye on City Hall.* So far, although coverage has been limited, Bill's personality has favorably impressed their editors, resulting in positive press. For example, the *Valley News* ran an editorial before the Republican primary that spoke so positively of Bill's energetic campaign that we are considering reprinting it as an ad.

Eye on City Hall has a peculiar history. It was created primarily as a vehicle to attack John Sullivan and was mailed to everyone

Advertisements like this appeared often in free weeklies.

FLASH

SCHEUERMAN CALLS FOR STEPS TO SAVE FAMILY FARMS
Meets With Senator Hoffmann to Discuss Issues

Bill Scheuerman, the Independent and Democratic candidate for the New York State Assembly, met recently with Senator Nancy Larraine Hoffmann. Hoffmann, the ranking minority member of the Senate Agricultural Committee and a leader in the fight to save the family farms, observed that Scheuerman has a clear understanding of the many problems facing central New York's farmers. "Bill Scheuerman," Senator Hoffmann stated, "will provide the farmers of Oswego County with the kind of aggressive leadership they need in the Assembly. Farmers will have a friend and an effective advocate in Bill Scheuerman."

Scheuerman thanked Senator Hoffmann for finding time from her busy schedule to discuss farm issues with him. "This shows how dedicated the Senator is to restoring the sanctity of the family farms," Scheuerman commented, "and I look forward to working with the Senator on these important issues."

Scheuerman's meeting with Senator Hoffmann is part of a series of conferences with elected officials knowledgable in agricultural affairs. Mr. Scheuerman has also met several times with Bill Parment, Chair of the Agriculture Committee in the Assembly. Scheuerman stated that the meetings represented an important step in resolving the many problems confronting Oswego's farmers. "High taxes, unfair regulations, and pressures from development have hurt our family farms," Scheuerman said. "Farming is Oswego's largest industry and we cannot afford to stand by and watch it die." High on Scheuerman's legislative agenda are property tax relief for farmers, legislation providing the right to farm, a review of the Department of Environmental Conservation's (DEC) regulations, and the need to find ways for DEC to respond more quickly to the needs of farmers.

Scheuerman stated that many of the issues discussed with Hoffmann and Parment were debated at the Farm Bureau's candidates forum in July. "At that forum I showed our farmers that agricultural issues are of primary importance to me," Scheuerman said. When elected Scheuerman wants to serve on the Agricultural Committee. "As a part of the Democratic majority, I will give farmers of Oswego County an effective voice in Albany," Sche in Oswego without charge. John has counterattacked, perhaps too vigorously, once going so far as to suggest an advertisers' boycott. Again, Bill's personality has helped him. Even though the paper ordinarily is staunchly Republican, its publisher interviewed Bill at length, and took a real liking to him. As a result, the paper has printed several of our press releases. Because of the primary, there have been interviews with Fran Sullivan and Mike Yerdon, with Bill's next week. However, each interview has been followed by a news story, based on one of our releases, portraying Bill quite favorably. Not all of these releases have been printed in a timely fashion (this week's was over a month old) but any positive publicity is good news for us. If Bill's interview turns out as favorably as he believes, we will be doing well.

Sunday, September 9

Our weekly meeting was productive. Our schedule for the remaining two months of the campaign is virtually complete. John Wilson has been working to schedule as many debates as possible, hoping to have at least one taped to televise on community access cable television. Our main fear is that Sullivan, who is not a very good speaker, will decline to appear. However, she has promised to debate. Any refusals will provide us with a useful issue. Sue Basualdo has been very thorough in scheduling meetings between Bill and local teachers. Bill's background, together with the NYSUT endorsement, has made public school teachers one of our best sources of support, especially since they are a politically concerned group with a high voter turnout. Jack, who was relatively quiet at this meeting, plans to take care of his school district in the town of Hannibal. Rand Bishop was supposed to be organizing an on-campus rally on October 1, but has yet to get started. We decided that he will make the physical arrangements and Greg Auleta and I will take care of the rest, primarily publicity.

We also worked on organizing leafletting and door-to-door campaigning in the most important towns and cities. Such traditional techniques are a must in our low budget campaign. We hope we have enough volunteers to get the job done. We also looked at some letters to different constituency groups. Don Wahrendorf, the Minetto Democratic committeeman, will go door-to-door distributing a letter urging people to vote for Bill. I drafted another fund-raising appeal to college faculty and staff, thanking them for their excellent response to our first letter but pointing out that we need still more assistance. Finally, with all petition challenges resolved, we will send a letter to all those who signed our independent petitions, thanking them and seeking their continued support. Many signed knowing little about Bill. They simply wanted to get him on the ballot so we will have to work to get them to vote for him. Although our campaign plans are pretty well set, implementation will not be so easy.

III. TWO CANDIDATES ON THE BALLOT

Tuesday, September 11

Bill delayed commuting to Albany until tomorrow in order to be available for interviews on primary day. We talked about how to approach the inevitable questions. Bill must ignore the temptation to take shots at the winner, who we expect to be Fran Sullivan. Because every story will focus on the primary winner, Bill must be prepared to take a secondary role for the day, avoiding the pettiness of partisan sniping. Instead, he should congratulate his main opponent and set out the major issues. He should state his hopes for a campaign centering on those issues, challenging the opposition to as many public debates as possible. Marc Heller's interview with Bill about a salary freeze indicated that my press release is beginning to have an impact. I hope Marc will hold his story until a day or two after the primary when it would have its greatest impact.

Bill and I then discussed some ideas for my next press release on crime. Without much enthusiasm, I told him it would have to include a sentence stating his support for the death penalty. Much more to both our liking were my other suggestions: a comprehensive reform of the entire criminal justice system to eliminate delays due to inefficiency without reducing constitutional rights; ensuring that punishment would be more certain and swift than under our current system; improved programs for crime victims to include better compensation, counseling, and consultation by prosecutors engaged in plea bargaining; improved drug education and job opportunities for young people; and making sure that white collar criminals will be punished more severely. Bill especially liked the last of these. My rhetoric stressed that S&L executives have cost us far more than all the bank robbers in the country and should not be let off more easily than their less privileged counterparts. Now all I have to do is figure out how to include all of this in a snappy release without making it too long.

As we expected and hoped, Fran Sullivan won the primary. Only about 6,500 Republicans turned out, giving her a nearly nine-hundred-vote margin. If Yerdon runs even a modest campaign on his independent line, he should take away a significant number of her votes in northern and western rural areas. There are also a number of Republicans who might switch to Bill out of resentment of her candidacy. Bill's radio interviews during election coverage were good. All the stations first ran a statement from Sullivan suggesting that she was building momentum and laying out taxes and spending as the main issues. Bill then congratulated her, stated that the voters need to decide who is best qualified regardless of party, and ended with the hope that they would be able to debate the issues. He also told one interviewer that Yerdon "has nothing to be ashamed of," and has also run a fine campaign. I know that this was aimed at picking off some of Yerdon's vote. Does this mean I am beginning to think like some crass politician or is it simply prudence?

Thursday night Greg and I will meet with a group of students. With Bill having been away from campus for three years, students need to get to know him all over again. If we can get him a lot of exposure, we know they will like him. But this may be neither easy nor enough. There is no galvanizing issue to get students excited enough to turn out on Election Day. Many are registered to vote in their parents' district rather than this one. The enthusiasm shown by these students who have promised to help could wane before the election as other concerns loom larger in their lives. We need to work hard to maintain enthusiasm for the next two months.

Greg has also been in touch with the Non-Traditional Student Union, whose president plans to come to our meeting. Because this group is older and has deeper roots in the community than other student organizations, convincing them to support Bill should result in a good number of votes. Too many people picture the typical college student as eighteen to twenty-one years old, having come to college directly from high school. But the percentage of older students has been growing phenomenally even in a small city like Oswego. The NTSU membership list includes 1,700 students, though many of these are inactive. Still, in a student body of 6,500 (full-time equivalent) students, it is a far more significant group than most people realize. These students are among the most motivated. If we can get their votes, we will have really accomplished something.

Thursday, September 13

No one was very surprised when neither Paul Austin nor the SA Vice-President showed up. Fortunately, those students who did come more than made up for the absentees. I began with an update on the campaign, including yesterday's endorsement by the local Labor Council, then tried as best I could to tell them something about Bill as well as why electing him would help all students. The students suggested we have our first rally at noon on October 1, a time when many students will pass by and inquire about what is going on. They will also set up a Students for Scheuerman organization to work on student registration, publicizing specific events, and generally getting the word out about who Bill is and why students should want to vote for him. We will help by speaking to student groups and providing such materials as literature, posters, bumper stickers, and our latest item—emery boards—which made a big hit at Karen's house. I am impressed by the students who came. They have some excellent ideas and their enthusiasm seems the sort that will be sustained.

Midway through the meeting Bill and John Wilson appeared, having promised to do so after the evening's campaigning at the Oswego Farmers' Market. Bill gave a brief, off-the-cuff talk about how he has addressed student concerns in the past and is continuing to do so. The students were particularly impressed by his work to reduce the proliferation of "nickel and dime" fees that SUNY has used to raise money. He provided the kind of detailed understanding of higher education issues that Frances Sullivan cannot. He also demonstrated a long record of work on these matters to back up his promises. Then John told us all that the first debate will take place on campus, organized by the student pre-law society, on October 4. This is great news for us and the students, provided they do a professional job and get a good turnout. We are pleasantly surprised that Sullivan accepted so quickly. On the other hand, the *Palladium Times* is shocked that they have been scooped in this fashion. This is not our fault; we offered them this date first but they held out for a later one, leaving them with the second debate as consolation for their red faces.

Bill drove in from Albany only for the evening's campaigning and our meeting. Early tomorrow morning he will make the three-hour drive back then return home again in the evening. Working, commuting, and campaigning at this pace requires an iron constitution as well as an outlook that I know Bill has but I admire nevertheless. How do candidates survive it? And why do they want to?

Wednesday, September 19

I was away this weekend but got home in time for some less than pleasing developments. Yerdon withdrew his independent candidacy, issuing a short statement that as a loyal Republican (an interesting comment from someone who has not only run for this office as a Democrat but also just opposed the party's endorsed choice in the primary) he is supporting Sullivan. He then made himself unavailable for further comment. His withdrawal will probably cost Bill between five hundred and 1,500 votes. Then I learned that Sullivan has pulled out of the campus debate. Whether this is part of a plan to avoid all debates or simply a belief that the college is Bill's home turf will soon become clear. It has to be a tough decision for her. Bill is likely to outdebate her if she agrees to joint appearances, but turning down invitations will cause people to wonder what she is afraid of. In the latter case, Bill could fairly state that he is running an issue-oriented campaign, ask the people to compare the positions of the two candidates, but point out that his opponent is unwilling to risk the comparison. Although hardly an original tactic, it could prove effective in a race between two candidates known only in parts of the county.

On the plus side, we are getting more coverage in the press even if progress has been extremely slow. Today, Marc Heller wrote a story about Bill's salary-freeze proposal, more than a week after he interviewed Bill about it. Overall, the story was positive, highlighting the proposal itself and Bill's willingness to make the "sacrifice" of living on a mere $57,000 plus expenses. Sullivan refused to make a similar commitment and called the proposal "grandstanding." Although it does have considerable elements of gimmickry, the proposal's purpose is to highlight a real frustration felt by the public at the selfishness of so many politicians. The salary freeze is a way to show sympathy with that frustration with a dramatic idea. Other papers printed Bill's release on farm issues, including a picture of him meeting with Senator Hoffman. It included highlights of their discussion of farm issues, several meetings between Bill and the Assembly Agriculture Committee chair, and Bill's agenda on important farm issues. I am amazed by how much Bill has learned on this subject. In fact, he has learned so well that he now suggests that if elected (or when elected, as he always puts it) he will seek a seat on the Agriculture Committee. Finally, the *Valley News* printed an article on the pig roast complete with quotes from Bill's speech, favorable comments on the size and enthusiasm of the crowd, and some positive words from Jack.

So far, our student supporters have chartered Students for Scheuerman, scheduled some dates to solicit support in the Student Union, and worked to publicize Bill in any way possible. Dave Glick's students run large public forums as part of a communications class, so Karen and Emilio have scheduled Bill to be one of the speakers at a forum on the First Amendment. It would be a far better topic for me but I am not running for office. Karen has proven to be an extremely conscientious intern, meeting with Jack almost daily. Whenever I get too cynical about students, some come along to restore my faith.

Saturday, September 22

Unconfirmed rumors have it that Yerdon withdrew after the Republicans promised to throw some business to his firm. Given the distaste that he has expressed for the way Sullivan was selected together with his minimal support for her, this seems plausible albeit impossible to verify. His brothers, with whom John Wilson has developed a friendly relationship, quietly told us that his organization will provide us with help in the towns where he has been strong. Anything that they do will help as we are quite weak there. Perhaps the withdrawal will not cost us so many votes after all.

My theme for this coming week will be job development. I tried to use the first couple of weeks of the official campaign for attention-getting secondary issues, hoping to save those of more substance for the phase of the campaign after the public became more aware of the election and the candidates. For Oswego County, jobs are a crucial issue. It is a relatively poor county, dependent upon agriculture and a few large industries such as Nestle, Miller Beer, SUNY, and Niagara Mohawk, the power company. Since

NiMo announced this week that it will lay off twelve hundred employees during the next three years, the timing for this subject is perfect, unfortunately. Bill's background as a political economist gives him demonstrable expertise. He has written a book about the steel industry and quite a few articles on economic issues, while much of his union work has touched on national and state economic problems. Yet when I talked to him, he had surprisingly little to suggest in the way of specific proposals. He pointed to his exhausting schedule of working and campaigning, saying it left him no time to develop substantive ideas. It reminds me of the scene at the end of the movie *The Candidate* when Robert Redford, having just defeated an incumbent Senator, takes aside his campaign manager and asks, "What do we do now?"

A political campaign, even one as low budget as ours, seems to leave no room to explore ideas. Instead, we communicate the notion that we share the concerns and values of the voters, who then must hope we will translate that concern into good public policy. Is it any wonder that the public is so often disappointed? Looking at the New York state legislature, we found little in the way of significant ideas for creating jobs. Everyone is so focused on the deficit that merely keeping the pork barrel half-filled is the substitute for real ideas. Bill's start-up theme of bringing the bacon to Oswego County makes it unlikely that our campaign against politics as usual will make more than a marginal improvement. Anyone seeking real change in the system must face up to the limits of electoral politics.

The theme of this week's press release is the state's failure to invest adequately in the future. New York's best asset is a trained work force, one that failures in education and job training risk losing. In Oswego County, we have wonderful natural resources as well so I want to stress that maintaining the environment is not only the right thing to do but also a business necessity. How to say this without getting bogged down in the details of economics is my next job.

Sunday, September 23

We never have quite the same people at our staff meetings. Today we added Doug Howell, our Fulton coordinator. Democrats often do well in Fulton, but Fran Sullivan comes from neighboring Volney. Her primary victory was largely due to a large majority in

Fulton, whose turnout exceeded the larger city of Oswego. Because of this, doing well in Fulton will take a great deal of work on our part. However, we have gotten only limited support from the city party organization, which seems more interested in two local races—one for City Court Judge, the other for Common Council. Thus, for now we have decided to put together our own organization. Doug is an interesting person to put in charge, a sixties radical from a family active in the Republican party. He returned to Fulton a few years ago after twenty years away. He is very enthusiastic, working hard to find those in the party willing to help us. Because he lacks confidence in his own contacts, we suggested several people in Fulton we think would be willing to help. Judging by his description of his activities and what others present had to say, he is doing a fine job. I told him so when the meeting broke up.

Bill and Jack were delayed because of a meeting of party VIPs at which Lou came under attack for not adequately supporting the party's candidates. They were pleasantly surprised by Mary Kay Dowd's vigorous criticism of the lack of party activity. This gained her some respect. Andy Hillman, who was at our meeting but had not even been notified of the party gathering, was unhappy about the slight.

Most of the meeting was devoted to details of scheduling events. Although we have pretty much completed Bill's schedule through the end of the campaign, enough flexibility has been left to add events such as debates. For each scheduled event we need to be sure that someone is in charge of the details. I suggested that Bill issue an open letter challenging Sullivan to name any place and time for a debate and he would be there. So far only one debate is set, conducted by the Oswego Press Club. And she may even duck out of that one. If so, Bill needs to point this out in as positive a way as possible.

We also talked about spending priorities—how to raise more money, what kinds of mailings to do, and advertising. We have quite a bit of old-fashioned paraphernalia to distribute—literature, buttons, bumper stickers, and signs. We have become a well-oiled machine.

Monday, September 24

The students have set up a booth in the student union to spread the word about Bill and get people registered. In the evening Greg and I met with Karen, Emilio, Paul Austin, and his V.P., Ed Cohen. On the positive side, Emilio and Karen drafted a letter asking students to register, explaining why they should vote for Bill, and plugging next week's campus rally. Greg will have five hundred made up for immediate distribution. Unfortunately, they have done little else to publicize the rally, so we have to work out some specific ways of doing so. It would be a disaster if only a few people attended. But even at this late date, we should be able to get a good crowd. An extra boost for us is that this morning the school paper interviewed Bill. With the interview appearing Thursday afternoon, the publicity (although Bill forgot to mention the rally during the interview) should make his name familiar enough for us to generate adequate attendance.

We also discussed getting a few volunteers for this weekend's city doorbell ringing and a late October fund-raiser for which Greg has already recruited a band and a bar. These student volunteers really want to help, but they need an occasional push. Karen and Emilio are getting academic credit, provided that they write satisfactory papers, but our other student volunteers are working primarily from idealistic motives. So it is not fair for me to be too hard on them. In fact, my only wish is to find more like them.

Sunday, September 30

I missed yesterday's doorbell ringing due to Yom Kippur. Although a lower than expected number of volunteers turned out (surely not everyone who failed to show up was Jewish!), the response in those parts of the city covered was excellent. We will simply expand our efforts, covering the rest of the city during the week. We will also be working on large mailings to potentially favorable voters during the next two weeks. With a low turnout likely due to Cuomo's expected landslide and Pierre Rinfret's disastrous campaign, winning the assembly race may come down to which side can best mobilize its supporters. At tonight's staff meeting we discussed how best to do this. We will need to get as many volunteers as possible to make phone calls. John Fitzgibbons donated a small phone bank in his office. With our limited budget we will need more such donations. We plan to rent a phone bank for the last few days of the campaign but its cost of thirty-five dollars per hour for twenty-two lines—which would be trivial for a big-budget effort—added up quickly for us. The staff meeting had quite a few new faces, in addition to John. Our volunteer effort is really expanding. This gives us hope that next weekend's doorbell ringing in Fulton will be adequately staffed.

Bill and John Wilson were late for the meeting due to a long and very positive meeting with Mike Yerdon's brothers. For the first time, Bill looked tired. His nonstop schedule is beginning to show. The Yerdons, who have a strong organization in the rural northern part of the county, have promised to do everything they can to help us. They believe that Bill is a far better candidate than his opponents. But they need to keep their efforts low key due to their brother's official endorsement of her. Their support is a significant advantage for us. There may not be a large number of voters in those towns but they are a strong part of the Republican majority. We hope that the Yerdons' support will move at least a few hundred Republican votes into our column.

Bill receiving the endorsement of the Yerdon family.

Monday, October 1

At first we thought the campus rally was a disaster. Few people showed up despite our student assistants' efforts. Students on our campus are simply not very excited about politics, especially without either national or statewide contests of great interest or any galvanizing issues. Fortunately, we scheduled Bill's speech during lunchtime so we were able to attract curious passersby. Bill spoke primarily about educational issues but brought up some others, including the environment and the overall state budget. The audience was appreciative, asking good questions. Many stopped to have a word with Bill. Despite the limited attendance considering the college's 6,500 students, just about all those who listened said they intend to vote for Bill, and a few left their names and addresses as volunteers. We also registered fifty new voters, as many as the Student Association registered all last year. A representative from one of the fraternities stopped by for information about registering his brothers. Our hopes of creating student interest in a year in which there have been dramatic budget cuts on a few SUNY campuses but not ours may have been unrealistic. Still, this was a modest success.

After the rally we stopped in at WRVO to speak with Chris Ulanowski, who is arranging the Press Club debate in Fulton. Because this is the only debate that Sullivan accepted, Bill will have to do well. He will also need to make as big an issue as possible of her failure to debate. In fact, she has made virtually no appearances before large groups, apparently because she is a poor speaker. If we can convey this to voters, we hope that they will ask themselves how she can represent Oswego County effectively if she is afraid to speak before any group larger or less friendly than the Republican party committee. Mike Yerdon may have let her get away with this, but to the extent we can do so without being overly nasty or negative, we must do everything possible to avoid it happening again. Bill is our greatest asset. We need to show people the difference between the two as much as possible. Our biggest hurdle is getting the media to cover the race.

Thursday, October 5

The routine tasks of an election campaign are dominating our time. On two evenings this week, volunteers addressed and stuffed envelopes with a mailing to registered voters who signed Mike Yerdon's independent petitions. With neither computers nor paid help available, we have to work the really old-fashioned way—by hand. Our radio ads are also primitive by today's standards, consisting essentially of conversations between Bill and John Wilson about issues and qualifications for office. Although we expect something slicker from the opposition, we have yet to see it. They have concentrated on newspaper ads so far but we expect a late blitz on the radio. Having doubled our limited advertising time starting this week, we are prepared. If we are able to raise more money, we hope to step things up still more during the final week. I wrote a newspaper ad summarizing some basic differences between the two candidates on issues of legislative salaries, the budget, education, and consumer protection. I make it clear that Bill has made specific proposals that he will fight for, while Fran Sullivan has yet to say much.

Keeping quiet and harvesting her normal vote was a successful strategy in the primary but we do not think it will work in the general election. If we are right, the one debate could be crucial for us. Because it will be in Fulton, we expect her side to try to pack the hall. To prevent this, we need to get about fifty of our supporters there to balance any cheering for her. On Sunday Bill and I will spend the morning discussing issues as well as going over the most effective arguments and how best to present them.

Student support is picking up. Appearing in this week's student newspaper were a column by Karen and Emilio and a letter from Andy Hillman (who is an alum) explaining why students should vote for Bill. The registration drive is gathering steam with help from student leaders who are resentful of the way Sullivan pulled out of the campus debate that was to have taken place today. Aiding our registration effort has been an upsurge of town-gown problems that have demonstrated the importance of politics to many students who live off-campus. Paul Austin has been going from one fraternity or sorority to another signing people up. Although city issues are the main reason for their interest, we believe that once they decide to vote in other elections, they will also look at the two assembly candidates and vote overwhelmingly for Bill. Several students who either heard Bill speak or heard about him from friends have approached me volunteering to help. In addition to citing the expected educational issues, some are impressed by what Bill says on other matters, particularly the environment. Idealism may not be thriving on our campus but there still is quite a bit waiting to be tapped if only more politicians would make the effort.

Sunday, October 7

The more the campaign progresses, the more optimistic we are. Bill and I tell each other that all candidates feel this way but we keep seeing unexpected positive signs that contradict our natural pessimism. This was the weekend for ringing doorbells in Fulton. With several prominent Republicans accompanying Bill in their wards and positive reactions from voters, our hopes of a solid majority in Fulton may have some foundation, especially now that the Fulton Democratic Party has begun to show enthusiasm for Bill's candidacy. Student registration has also started to take off. In the last off-year elections only fifty students voted on campus. Probably another seventy-five or so voted off campus. Thus, when Karen walked into the Board of Elections on Friday with 250 registration forms, the Republican official she gave them to had a look of shock. With another week to go, we expect to give her another surprise. The Republicans have scheduled their own candidate forum on campus but we do not expect Sullivan to cause much excitement. Bill will be making some more appearances on campus to generate enthusiasm.

Bill and I worked on the debate. I gave him a two-page single-spaced paper summarizing approaches to issues and suggesting how to present his arguments and get across his themes. After John joined us about halfway through, we discussed possible questions and pitfalls for a couple of hours. Next Sunday we will try a mock debate in preparation for the real thing the following Wednesday. We are hoping to put enough heat on Sullivan to make her accept more debates.

Much of the meeting concentrated on our "get out the vote" drives. We have completed most of our mailings and are beginning to make phone calls to potential supporters. We arranged times to rent a phone bank for the last days of the campaign and put the finishing touches on Bill's schedule, which now has virtually no free time. We hope that the union endorsements that are still coming in will bring in enough money to pay for additional radio and newspaper ads and help our "get out the vote" effort. Turnout for Bill's fund-raiser next Saturday looks like it will be good. In addition we have a band and a location for a student fund-raiser at two dollars per person on October 18. Except for Mike, all of the Yerdon family is in our corner with public endorsements about to come out. John and Ambrose Yerdon have been working hard in areas where we previously had very little organizational strength. I keep wanting to pinch myself but I really think we can win. As Bill said to me today, echoing Robert Redford in *The Candidate,* what will we do then? He was kidding, but all jokes have at least a kernel of seriousness in them.

Saturday, October 13

Bill's fund-raiser tonight was a great success, netting over two thousand dollars. More than sixty people came for cocktails at twenty-five dollars each and about two-thirds stayed for dinner at another twenty-five dollars. Bill is anxious about an interview by a reporter who appeared to be hostile (the article will appear tomorrow) but we keep reassuring him. He has to be willing to shrug off an occasional bad story. The fact that we decided not to take a poll in order to use our more limited resources elsewhere means that we have no objective measurement of how well we are doing. In a way, this is good. Poor poll results at this stage would be discouraging without enabling us to do anything differently. Our strategy was so obvious from the beginning, given our situation and resources, that there is little a poll could tell us except how well we are doing. Good poll results would provide only a momentary boost for morale. We just have to play the cards we were dealt.

The fund-raiser provided the morale boost we needed. We had a truly diverse group of people—college faculty and staff, political leaders like Jim McMahon and the Yerdons, dependable campaign volunteers, local labor leaders, a number of community leaders, and a few more people. The Basualdos did a magnificent job of putting everything together, even arranging to have their two children, Bill's daughter Liesel and one of her friends, and Nancy Weber's daughter running around serving hors d'oeuvres during cocktails and coffee after dinner. Everyone worked hard for a wonderful payoff. The money raised, together with that provided by the unions backing Bill, will provide us with enough for a late advertising blitz.

Sunday, October 14

Bill's fears about the article in the Oswego section of today's Syracuse newspaper turned out to be unfounded. My guess is that Bill jumped to conclusions when the reporter, Joel Broadway, merely pressed him the way a journalist should. With only about three weeks left we are all getting jumpy. The newspaper ran adjoining stories about Bill and Fran Sullivan. Fran has begun to contradict herself. That should help us a great deal. Her former position on abortion was that she would only allow it for rape and incest and to save the life of a pregnant woman; now she favors current New York law that is pro-choice with no restrictions. She said she will reduce spending but later in the article stated that she favors increased spending on education, police, health care, and several other programs. She also came out in favor of a proposal to have Route 481 bypass Fulton. This could cost her support there, especially among the business community, which would be devastated if the highway no longer went through the city. Bill has been cautious on this issue, arguing for an expert evaluation of the economic impact before any state action. What makes it tricky is that many people in Oswego like the bypass, creating a conflict between the two cities.

The article about Bill was accurate and objective. The one problem was its oversimplification of Bill's position on the Department of Environmental Conservation. The DEC has become a large entrenched bureaucracy that often favors, as Bill frequently puts it, "the big guy over the little guy." Bill seeks to streamline it to return to its mission—protecting the environment. The article translated this to mean that Bill simply wants to cut the DEC. As a result, he was really hassled at a Greenpeace rally. What made this ironic was that the major criticism came from a woman with whom he has fought for the environment for fifteen years. She admitted that she has little faith in that particular reporter but paid no real attention to Bill's attempts to explain his position or point to his record. Finally, he took the only way out he could, asking her to look at his opponent and think about what electing her would do.

During the afternoon Gene Basualdo, John Wilson, Jack Tyrie, Bill, Louise, and I worked on the debate. Bill wrote a good opening statement that he delivered to us. It was fortunate that we decided to keep the group small because the five of us kept giving suggestions simultaneously. We managed to get organized enough to craft a good statement that gets across Bill's major themes, tells something about him as a person, and draws contrasts between him and his opponent. Surprisingly, the opening statement remained coherent and organized. We spent less time on specific issues, having done that the previous week with several follow-ups since. The closing statement depends somewhat on what happens in the debate. Bill is quick enough to be able to handle that provided he has a few basic themes prepared.

Our evening meeting was devoted primarily to "get out the vote" efforts organized by Jim Clemens. Though voter registration lists were available from the party, they did not include telephone numbers. Neither the party nor any of its candidates had a county-wide list of phone numbers, even of registered Democrats. Even the few town leaders who had such lists had not updated them for several years.

To rectify this situation, Jim has organized a group effort to look up these tens of thousands of phone numbers. He has a hand-ful of phone lines to make early contacts with voters in order to discover those favorable enough to call on election day and those leaners or undecideds we need to send literature to. Each caller is given a script to work from. Jim plans to concentrate on Oswego and Fulton, a huge job, with additional work done from people's homes and smaller operations in the towns. The Yerdon brothers and a few others will take care of the northern rural areas. The teachers' union, NYSUT, will make phone calls to their members on October 29 and 30 from Syracuse, and we will supply additional volunteers. For the days before the election we have rented a phone bank for a more centralized operation.

On election day the poll watchers will tell us who has and who has not voted, allowing us to call potential voters to remind them to vote and to provide rides or baby sitters if necessary. This is a real old-fashioned political organization but it is necessary if we are to have a chance. The party organization used to do this routinely; we have to do it ourselves. Because we expect a low turn-out, the election might be won by the side that does the best job of mobilizing its supporters. It is a daunting task but we think we can do it.

Wednesday, October 18

Tonight's debate was our big opportunity. It was standing room only in the hall as cameras taped the event, which will air tomor-row night on cable access. Most of the debate went just as we hoped. Bill was confident, positive, and knowledgeable. Fran was tentative and extremely nervous. She had so little to say that she passed on many of her rebuttals. Bill was particularly good on his

88

opposition to building incinerators. Fran said she supported them because they had been declared safe. But Bill was able not only to cite dangers, but also to point to incinerators previously declared safe that turned out not to be. He then suggested alternatives. Fran tried blaming all of the state's fiscal woes on the Democrats in state government, but Bill persuasively argued that with the Republicans controlling the state senate, the two parties shared responsibility. He preferred solving the problem to the politically expedient tactic of blaming the opposition. He was able to point to specific accomplishments such as forming a bipartisan coalition of Town Supervisors that kept a toxic waste dump out of the county; she was able only to point to her wonderful late husband and her party positions. As best we could tell, Fran has never held a full-time paid job.

All of this turned out to matter little. Instead, the debate was dominated by Fran's shocking final statement in which she suddenly turned negative with a barrage of charges that made little sense. Of course, she and her advisers must have known this, or else why wait until a final statement that Bill was not permitted to rebut. Actually, we were lucky she went last, because Bill did not scrap his own close for an angry point-by-point rebuttal. It also made her tactics quite transparent to everyone there. Her major charges were that during a financial crisis Bill went on leave from SUNY (implying he was getting paid twice) and that during his leave "he sued the State University for an increase in salary," making his proposed salary freeze for the legislature hypocritical. When questioned after the debate, she backtracked, claiming that this alleged lawsuit was actually a grievance (she had trouble distinguishing between the two) and that she had learned of this from a "high-placed source at the college." Probably the best response would have been laughter but we needed to make sure that the press realized the absurdity of her charges.

Bill's leave was unpaid, allowing the state to replace him with a more junior, lower-salaried faculty member. Since the state was not paying him, he could hardly have filed a grievance asking for more pay. During past union struggles, he sometimes fought against the administration, leading to a grievance several years ago.

Even if the charge were true, what would its relevance be? Was she saying that no one who ever asked for a raise as a private citizen could oppose an increase for legislators? Surely she understood that public officials are different from private citizens in their duties and obligations. Those genuinely undecided at the debate and even a few Republicans who had been leaning in her favor were appalled by her tactics. I was sitting next to Louise, who was naturally very angry. Bill was just as angry but he had to restrain it in order to take the high road. While Fran engaged in mud slinging, Bill stuck to the issues and qualifications, speaking in as positive a manner as possible. How it is covered by the media will be crucial. After I got home, Marc Heller, unable to reach Bill, called me. I discussed the allegations and explained grievances and other union matters to him.

Thursday, October 18

Most of the news coverage was as expected. WGES radio began by discussing some of the substantive issues, then talked about Fran's charges, pointing out that Bill did not have an opportunity to reply. The station also explained his post-debate rebuttal. Marc made the charges the lead, headlining his article "Sullivan's charge tinges Assembly campaign with bitterness." He explained what she said, then analyzed the charges, occasionally referring to "a Scheuerman campaign staff member familiar with union grievances." I had not really expected to be famous. The unfortunate aspect of the coverage, however, was that Bill's excellent performance and all the significant issues were obscured by the coverage of this artificial controversy.

Meanwhile, Bill spoke to a group of merchants in Fulton about the bypass. The mayor, Muriel Allerton, is going to speak in support of Bill's position. However, Oswego's mayor, John Sullivan, favors the bypass. Bill simply wants to go slow to be careful about ensuring that Fulton is not hurt too badly. We hope he can maintain this balance for the next couple of weeks. In the evening we had a student fund-raiser. Greg arranged for a band to donate its services (although we paid them a little from the money we raised) and for a local bar owner to donate his establishment as long as he kept the bar receipts. Charging two bucks per person meant that we did not raise much money, but our main goal was to generate some enthusiasm. The band was great, turnout was large, and Bill circulated and gave a brief, energetic speech. We are pleased with the results.

Fran, on the other hand, made her one-and-only appearance on campus—with other Republican candidates—at a Young Republicans meeting last Monday. The audience was quite small—

according to the local paper, candidates practically outnumbered students – and included Paul Austin and Ed Cohen who appeared in a show of bipartisanship. Today's coverage in the campus paper is unlikely to gain Fran any votes. When Ed Cohen asked her about her stand on the bill to stiffen penalties against bias-related violence, an important issue on a campus on which several bias-related incidents recently occurred, she replied that she had not heard of it. She also supported a tuition increase. When it was pointed out that a two hundred dollar increase could cause a 3 percent enrollment drop, her answer, according to the article, was "Then there will be a way for them to matriculate."

We hope to continue to show the contrast between the two candidates on issues of interest to students. My letter urging students to vote for Bill because of his long history of fighting for SUNY also appeared in the campus paper. In addition, I have written a press release on the anti-bias bill, which Bill supports. I plan to have it distributed to the campus media and student government leaders. Bill will appear as a panelist at Tuesday's National Issues Forum on the press and politics. This will give him both additional campus exposure and a chance to meet with reporters participating in and covering the event. To ensure a large student vote we plan to put an ad in the final *Oswegonian* before the election and to have our student interns contact registered students on election day and remind them to vote.

Saturday, October 20

Bill's schedule, already exhausting, will be stepped up during the remaining couple of weeks before the election. Highlights are the Moose Lodge tonight and the American Legion and Nestle chocolate workers (who have endorsed Bill) tomorrow. Because Fran Sullivan's qualifications are so weak, our strategy of contrasting the two by direct appearances coupled with limited advertising and a few mailings seems to be working. Bill has taken an independent stance, criticizing both parties and attacking politics as usual; he repeats a theme of protecting the average person, including traditional Republican interests such as small business and farmers as well as the normal Democratic labor and city vote; and he avoids the common Democratic pitfalls of being seen as soft on crime or in favor of more taxes and spending. The Republicans are having trouble finding a theme to counter him. I think this explains Fran's debate strategy. More puzzling is the fact that we have had no competition in advertising for the last month with only a few Sullivan print ads. I am sure there will be a real blitz on the radio during the next two weeks, but we have taken all the money we can spare to step up our advertising.

We also have to get the free media to pay more attention to the campaign. Bill called Marc Heller, resulting in a nice interview yesterday in which he promised to continue an issue-oriented campaign without mud-slinging. He drew a contrast between his and Sullivan's approaches to running for office and challenged Fran to debate again. He also got Chris Ulanowski to accompany him as he campaigned in a supermarket parking lot. Because the location gives him an opportunity to stress consumer issues (especially his views on scanners and the item pricing law) and the reception has generally been quite friendly, these are among Bill's favorite stops. Because several people spontaneously told him how turned off they were by Sullivan's debate performance, we expect a good story during the week. Chris wants to interview both candidates first, ensuring either a fairly lengthy piece or several shorter ones on WRVO radio.

IV. STRETCH DRIVE: THE LAST TWO WEEKS

Saturday, October 27

Today was the county Democrats' big fund-raiser. Geraldine Ferraro was the draw. First she spoke on campus. For a Saturday morning talk scheduled on short notice, the turnout was incredible, probably a couple of hundred people. Ferraro gave a short talk about her political career, then took questions on both personal and political issues. Her pleasant, sometimes funny, low-key recollections were well received. I got a chance to talk to her and found her quite friendly. She has been traveling all over New York state to enhance her prospects for a 1992 Senate race against Al D'Amato. She told us that her decision will be made after a January poll. At noon, she went to the party fund-raiser for a brief appearance. With 120 people there, as well as television coverage from Syracuse and the usual local media, the luncheon appears to have been a great success. We hope that some of the money raised (at twenty-five dollars per person) will be given to the party's candidates. Our campaign needs it desperately. We have raised about $18,000 but spent about $20,000. Fortunately, we have already bought our last week of radio and newspaper advertising but are anxious to do more. We have been promised some union money, which will at least pay off some of our current obligations. It would be a shame for Bill to have to dig into his own pocket, although a post-election fund-raiser could cover some costs, probably all, if Bill wins.

Bill has kept up his usual hectic schedule. To counter it, Fran Sullivan's advertising has kicked in. She even ran radio ads on the Syracuse stations, something we are unable to afford. Although hers were professionally produced, I do not find them more effective than our self-made ads.

Finally the news media, especially the newspapers, are expanding their coverage. When we ran an ad showing all the Yerdon family except Mike supporting Bill, it generated several newspaper stories. My former student, Tim Sheridan, asked both Bill and Fran for fifteen-minute interviews on his Sunday morning radio show. He now has a better time slot, 8:30, so Bill gladly accepted. WKIX-FM, a Syracuse popular music station with a significant audience in Oswego County, gave Bill a rare chance to get on Syracuse radio. Fran is so poor at such interviews that she declined even a free one. The result was a very good half hour interview in which Tim pointed out three times that Sullivan had declined an invitation. The interview will air the Sunday before the election. For our money-starved campaign, this is a break.

Sunday, October 28

At tonight's meeting everyone had positive feedback from campaign activities. A surprising number of prominent Republicans has told one or another of us that they will back Bill. Carol Dwyer had a reception at her house in the town of Mexico at which thirty-five people, more than half of them Republicans, greeted Bill with expressions of support. Our signs have sprouted all over the place. Rumor has it that the Republicans have taken a poll showing Sullivan ahead in Fulton but giving Bill a 2–1 edge in Oswego. The details made the poll sound unreliable—a small sample taken several weeks ago—but if the Oswego figures are anywhere near that, we can win. Even the Fulton figures give us reason to be optimistic since they were taken before Sullivan's advocacy of the bypass.

Entering the final two weeks, we have to concentrate on getting our vote out. The Yerdons are well organized in the northern part of the district and have already begun making calls. At the meeting, several of the people from Fulton indicated that the party there is prepared for calling potential voters on election day and getting them to the polls. Unfortunately, with no similar organization in Oswego we are on our own. We have to put together our own organization in the city and town of Oswego. Jim Clemens has already begun making phone calls from a donated office. On Election Day, operations will be transferred to a rented phone bank on campus. We have lined up people to make calls, runners to bring lists to and from polling places to let us know who has not yet voted, and drivers to provide rides to the polls. In a couple of the towns, there is a local party committee to do this. In most of the others, we have some volunteers who are willing to take on the job. Jack, who has been involved in nearly all legislative races during the past ten years, assures us that this is the first time a Democratic candidate has had such an extensive organization. We know that the Republicans are organized too, so we have to outwork them to win.

Tomorrow evening I am going to Liverpool to make phone calls to teachers from a phone bank supplied by NYSUT. Tonight we worked on a short script for the calls. We have plenty of volunteers for Monday but need more for Tuesday, a day that I have an impossible teaching schedule. Greg and I intend to do some recruiting with a few late phone calls. Saturday as many of us as possible will try to cover the city of Oswego with a literature drop. We tried this a few weeks ago but were unable to cover the whole city. This time we have already lined up thirty people with more to come so we hope to be more efficient. Some of our volunteers in the towns have been doing the same thing. Nancy Weber has been incredible, driving to all sorts of isolated areas to distribute literature. With this literature distribution, a targeted mailing, our late advertising campaign, and our "get out the vote" drive we expect to get our message across. It is pretty old-fashioned but we think it will work. During our meeting we mused about how much easier Bill's reelection campaign will be.

Wednesday, October 31

Our calls to NYSUT members could not have gone better. Each of the two nights we had a dozen volunteers calling the 2,400 teachers in Oswego County. One of the nice things about calling teachers is that many have taken the time to read the literature that we sent them and liked what they read. For many, simply the fact that Bill is a teacher is enough. Others like his background and experience and his issue positions, confirmed by the union endorsement. Only two of the people told us that they are voting for Sullivan, although no doubt some of those who politely said they have not yet made up their minds simply did not want to offend the caller. Most important to us is the enthusiasm with which so many expressed their support. We are certain that this will translate into many votes.

Unfortunately, Fran's negative ads have kicked in: Bill was born in New York City, he went to school in New York City, he is a tax and spend liberal, etc. Her monetary edge is showing. They are running on all the local radio stations and on Syracuse radio as well. We knew that this would happen but it was still painful when it did. On the one hand we cannot make Dukakis's mistake and let the ads go unanswered, but on the other we cannot spend all of our time replying to charges. Striking the right balance will not be easy but it has to be done. One indication of the problems we face was a conversation I had with Marc Heller. Once again we went over Bill's 1981 salary. I asked Marc why he was dwelling on such irrelevancies at great length when there were important issues that needed to be discussed. His response was something like, "Well, you know Fran is not very good at that." For heaven's sake, I replied, isn't it important for voters to see that? Present her views to them and let them judge her grasp of the subject. Politics can be an exasperating business, all right.

Thursday, November 1

Marc's story was not bad since it quoted from many neutral people refuting Fran's charges. Bill counterattacked, stating that their falsity shows her poor judgment. Unfortunately, Marc's paper endorsed Fran for the most frivolous of reasons. Despite admitting that Bill is more qualified, the editorial stated that being born in the county makes her closer to the constituency and that Bill is somehow tainted by his ties to SUNY. Apparently her lack of any experience is a great asset. In the words of the editorial, Fran was endorsed, "not because she's more qualified, but because she would come into office with fewer distractions." I had to remind myself of all the studies showing what little impact editorials have.

Bill's defense is to rationalize by noting that when the *Fulton Patriot* once endorsed a Democrat for mayor, it lost $50,000-worth of advertising. Perhaps that precedent influenced what the *Pal-Times* claimed was a close decision this time. We do have an ace in the hole: the *Oswego Valley News*. Despite rarely endorsing candidates (one every five years or so), it gave Bill a ringing endorsement, comparing him favorably to Abe Lincoln. Had we written it ourselves, we would have toned it down.

Because Fran is outspending us by a large margin, one possible response is to publicize the difference, arguing that Bill is going directly to the people while she is afraid to debate or be interviewed, preferring to buy ads and hurl mud. At this late date we have to stick with our basic strategy—that Bill is a different candidate who gets things done rather than pointing fingers, that he will fight for the average voter, that he is indebted to no one. We have to make the most of the cards dealt to us. So far, we have done much better than anyone expected. The Republicans' negative tactics may be evidence of just how well. Still, it would be awfully nice to have the money to run a more media-oriented campaign.

I have been thinking about how much my attitude has changed since we began the campaign last summer. Then I was able to view the silliness of it all with wry detachment: now despite an even greater amount of nonsense, I find myself too involved to laugh at these ironies. The day-to-day pressures make it hard to see the big picture. If this is happening to me, how much more so it must be for Bill. I need to provide an anchor (my metaphors are getting a bit out of hand) to keep him from overreacting to attacks, no matter how foolish they are. Bill is exceptionally lucky to have Louise. She provides a steadiness and reliability that we have come to take for granted. She has put in nearly as much time and surely as much worry as he has, albeit in less visible ways.

In the past, when students asked me why I did not run for political office, I replied glibly that I would never be able to make the kind of compromises necessary to have a chance of election. As I watch Bill, I realize just how true that answer is. Even if I had the ability to duplicate his energy and his likability (I tend to be more the curmudgeonly type), I could never trim my sails the way he has. I love a good argument too much. I also often tell myself that the only thing that I have that no one can take from me is my integrity. Yet I cannot fault Bill. Facing the limits of our system of elections, he is doing the best he can to achieve some good. Benjamin Ginsberg put the paradox well: "Even when, rightly or wrongly, the study of voting seemed to suggest that what voters decided was unlikely to have much significance for a government's actions, students of voting continued to think that somehow it should."

Friday, November 2

One payoff of our volunteer campaign is showing up in the letters to the editor columns of the newspapers. So many of us have written letters that they have become almost a regular feature. Yet the variety of writers shows that it is not simply a few campaign staffers. Yesterday, a letter from Mike Yerdon for Sullivan was surrounded by positive letters about Bill from Marie Austin, Francis McKeown (a Republican from Fulton), and Howard Rose, a member of the town board in Sullivan's hometown of Volney. Today's *Pal-Times* had one from Bill summing up what he has learned from all of his campaigning, and what he promises to do if elected; one from me asking about contradictions in Fran's positions on abortion and government spending as well as why she opposes a salary freeze; and a third from Paul Zurek explaining why Bill would be the more effective legislator. We also ran a nice print ad showing Bill meeting with Mike Bragman. It explained how being a member of the majority party in the Assembly has made Mike more effective in getting state money for his district. It also noted that Bill was recently endorsed by the firefighters union. The connection between these two points was Bragman's ability to get significant state support for volunteer firemen while Ray Chesbro could not do the same for Oswego County. Emilio also wrote a nice profile of Bill as a feature in the college paper.

We have started to hear about negative reaction to Fran's attack ads. Judging how widespread such reactions are is difficult, as those who like the ads are unlikely to contact us. Nevertheless, many Republicans, including some officeholders, are among those complaining and assuring us of their support; this gives us reason to be optimistic. Oswego County is old-fashioned enough not to approve of the kind of attacks that would be considered fairly mild elsewhere. In addition, Fran has not really created a positive image for herself to counter Bill's. We also learned that one of our graduate school professors held a small fund-raiser for us in his New York City bar. Although the check is only for $150, it is a real morale booster and will pay for a late newspaper ad. On our budget, every dollar counts.

Saturday, November 3

The last weekend of the campaign will be crunch time. We have to be prepared for all sorts of rumors from the opposition. Even though I hope such fears are exaggerated, it never hurts to be prepared. Today, a letter to the editor had an out-of-context quote from Bill's book in favor of worker ownership, making him appear to be—gasp!—a socialist. We just have to grin and bear such things. In this case, all Bill had said was that when plants were closed as unprofitable, giving the workers a chance to buy them would be better than abandonment. I would hate to have to go back and defend everything I ever put into print. Another reason for me not to run for office.

Testiness in our camp has begun to pop up. Andy Hillman is upset that we ran an ad in *Eye on City Hall* since its main reason for existence seems to be to attack Mayor Sullivan. For us, however, it was a good investment. It was mailed to every household in the city, very good coverage for a small amount of money. Despite their attacks on some Democrats, they have been more than fair to Bill, printing as many of our releases as Fran's as well as an interview that was no less friendly than the one with her. Apparently, Jack and Lou also had some words, although neither Bill nor I was there. I suspect it was because we have not been pushing Mario Cuomo's candidacy as hard as Lou would like. Mario will win reelection easily whatever we do, but he is not terribly popular in this county (although Pierre Rinfret is even less so). We made this decision because Bill wanted to remain free to criticize the governor when the two disagree. Not only was that the honest thing to do, it underlined Bill's independence, helping to attract the independent and Republican votes we need to win. At this point of the campaign season, we are all a bit tired. I doubt these disagreements will mean anything.

One last big job was distributing leaflets to everyone in the city of Oswego. Inside our pamphlet we inserted a reprint of the *Valley News* endorsement. It is actually more favorable than some of our own literature yet comes from a more credible source. The *Pal-Times* endorsement is so equivocal that Fran cannot do the same with it. We had more than twenty volunteers first inserting the reprints by hand and then going to a neighborhood and distributing them. With a population of 20,000, Oswego was small enough to cover in one day with a lot of work. Fortunately, it was a beautiful Indian summer day. We started at 9:00 A.M., quietly slipping literature under doors so as not to wake people up. While our group of volunteers covered the city, others worked in a few of the more important towns. We covered Fulton last weekend, and other towns at various times during the last two weeks. Overall, the reaction has been friendly with a few people asking questions and many more volunteering positive comments.

Except for our "get out the vote" drive and a few more personal appearances by Bill, there is not much left for us to do except worry and wait for the results. Whatever happens, we have a lot to be proud of. We have worked very hard, changing a candidacy that few outside the campaign gave much of a chance to a credible one with a real shot at victory despite a deficit of 2-1 in registration and nearly 3-1 in spending.

Sunday, November 4

In our last staff meeting, there was little for us to discuss. Tomorrow we plan to do some last-minute literature distribution in a few towns, make some calls to get out the vote, and send out John Wilson in a sound truck to get the word out. Election Day will be a lengthy affair, starting at 6:00 A.M., when we distribute our voting lists to the Democratic election inspectors as the polls open. The rest of the day will be devoted to getting out our voters. Jack and Jim Clemens will go to the Board of Elections to get the count. Then we will move on to the celebrations. Bill and Louise will spend half an hour in Fulton before returning to Oswego.

We hope that planning the post-election celebration is not an omen. Since the party did not arrange anything, we set up our own affair at the steamfitters union headquarters. Because Lou got around to making his own arrangements only a few days ago, there will be two parties. Bill and Louise will stop briefly at Lou's, then finish up at ours.

Once all of these details were worked out, Bill gave us a pep talk, thanking everyone for working so hard and expressing guarded optimism. Ron Patrick and Ann and Tom Dann from the Fulton party expressed satisfaction with the situation there. Of course, this was the time for optimism but, as that most tired of political clichés tells us every year, the only poll that counts will be on Election Day. When you are a part of a campaign you tend to hear the best news; the negative is heard by the opposition. Every candidate is thus lulled into false optimism by the friendly faces encountered along the way. Whenever Bill or I begin to get too optimistic, we remind one another that Barry Goldwater was lulled into a similar frame of mind after every 1964 speech.

Tuesday, November 6

The big day finally arrived. After my last class, I headed to our phone bank. The operation was very impressive. About thirty volunteers were working as people came and went with lists of those who had already voted. As each list came in, the names were scratched off our master list. The master list was then assigned to someone, who called the remaining Democrats as well as independents who previously had been called and identified as potential supporters. This list would be a crucial tool for future efforts to organize the Democratic Party. We called thousands of people in the city and town of Oswego. By 8:00 P.M. we closed up shop in

Watching election results (including son Karl on far right).

a state of exhaustion. The polls closed in another hour, and there was nothing left to do. We scattered briefly, eventually to reunite at our Election Night party.

A small group was there when I arrived at 9:00. The waiting was torture, even for a short time. We passed the time by making predictions, trading campaign anecdotes, and discussing early results in other states. Nancy Weber, who has been as dependable as any volunteer could be, asked, "What are we going to do to fill our Sunday nights now that there won't be any staff meetings?" Not having seen Ray Peterson for a while I asked him how he has been, discovering that he had a horrendous summer; several members of his family had health problems. Happily, everyone was better, but he had confined his campaign work to the area he lived in, which explains why I had not seen him lately.

As the early returns began to trickle in, it became clear that Bill was going to lose. Despite the band, refreshments, and a now large group of people who were normally very lively, all enthusiasm disappeared. We tried to convince one another that we ran a good race, that there were was little we could have done better, that given the nature of the district we should be proud to have come so close. Bill did better than any Democrat in the last twenty years in a district that the party has won once in the last one hundred years. The results came in: Sullivan 16,600 to Scheuerman's 13,200. Bill ran well ahead of the rest of the ticket. The gubernatorial returns: Conservative Herbert London 11,800, Cuomo 9,800, and Rinfret 9,100. We won every district in the city of Oswego, narrowly carried Fulton, and won in the towns of Minetto and Oswego. Unfortunately, this was not enough to overcome heavy losses in the rural towns. Despite Nancy Weber's hard work, our hopes for cutting into the Republican farm vote did not work out.

Bill seemed to be taking his loss well. He got up to give us all a pep talk. "When we started we knew how to count," he began. He thanked everyone who worked so hard on his behalf, then vowed to continue to work to build a real Democratic party. Lou was nowhere to be found, not only at our event but also at his own. I imagined him taking the call from state party chair John Marino about the governor's getting less than a third of the vote in the county. All of us reassured one another, wishing each other well. No doubt we will be back at work together in one way or another. Bill and Louise will hold a thank-you party at their house on Saturday. Next week they will take a well-deserved vacation in the Bahamas.

Conclusion

The official election results were Sullivan 16,987 and Scheuerman 13,344.[1] The obvious reaction for any losing campaign is to ask what went wrong. Yet even thinking about such a question tells us a great deal about this type of campaign. Even though the winner's margin of 3,643 votes was the closest in many years, the 56 to 44 percent result was essentially the same as the previous open seat contest between Chesbro and Yerdon in 1980. Therefore, it is far more productive to ask why there was so much optimism on our part during the campaign.

To answer this question we must first understand what the expectations were when Bill first received the party's endorsement, then explore the dynamics of the campaign.

The introduction suggested that deciding whether to run is one of the most difficult choices made by any political activist as well as one that is least understood by scholars. Bill's decision was made more out of a belief that running would be a positive experience for himself and a chance to raise important issues than out of an expectation of getting elected.[2] However, realism about the likelihood of victory was balanced against the hope that, if somehow everything went right, victory was possible. There seemed to be concrete reasons for qualified optimism. The party ticket was headed by a governor expected to win reelection overwhelmingly; the Republicans were likely to nominate a little-known candidate who would face a divisive primary fight that might even result in a third-party candidacy by a disgruntled loser; and there was a potential student vote, a new source of support that had never been tapped. In the end, none of these factors affected the outcome. Even though Governor Cuomo was reelected, he was not very popular in Oswego County, finishing second to Conservative Herb London. Rather than pulling in votes for Bill, Cuomo ran

103

12 percent behind him. Although there was a Republican primary, Michael Yerdon quickly halted his independent race and endorsed Fran Sullivan. Finally, the student vote never materialized. A separate on-campus election district that included about half of the student body was won by Bill by a margin of 58–27 votes, a more than 2–1 edge but an insignificant total of eighty-five votes. Considering that about 3,000 students live in this district, the result was extremely discouraging.

Yet somehow the realism shown at the beginning of the campaign was replaced by a growing optimism. Viewed objectively and after the fact, such optimism seems little more than self-delusion. Not only were party registration and past election results overwhelmingly in favor of the Republican Party, their candidate outspent Bill by $55,487 to $19,386.[3] It also was clear that at least two of the three potential advantages mentioned in the previous paragraph were not going to help. Even without polls, our political intelligence made it obvious that the governor was in trouble in Oswego County. Yerdon's endorsement of Sullivan also took place not long after the primary. Yet, as those potential positives evaporated, we found others to take their place. This was true despite the fact that Bill and I, as political scientists, were so aware of the dangers of misplaced optimism that we continually reminded ourselves not to take positive signs too seriously. Even if that was not enough, it is clear that all candidates, with the possible exception of those who are on the ballot but do not make a serious effort, will strongly overestimate their chances of victory.

One principle of political campaigns, even those that seem hopeless underdogs, must be: *No matter what setbacks a campaign suffers, the candidate and his/her organization tend to perceive their prospects of success as increasing as the election grows nearer.* This rule seems most applicable to volunteer-based campaigns, for they have the greatest psychological stake in the success of their candidates. They are also the least likely to be able to afford regular polls that could serve to temper their optimism. Even such objective evidence is not always sufficient to overcome the strong tendency of our rule. In 1972, when every survey, including his own, made it obvious that George McGovern was going to lose the presidential election overwhelmingly to incumbent Richard Nixon, McGovern told one reporter that after seeing discouraging poll results, "I'd get out among the people, you know, and you'd see a different thing. You'd see that there were really masses of people who wanted a fundamental change."[4]

It could hardly be otherwise. Volunteers are motivated to work hard for no tangible reward by this belief that they are making progress. This provides much of the answer to one of the questions posed in the introduction: how morale remains high within the candidate's volunteer organization. Voters who contact the campaign are overwhelmingly favorably disposed to it. Those likely to vote for the opposition will often give a noncommittal or even positive answer so as not to offend campaign workers with whom they are likely to have only brief contact. The cumulative impact of such positive comments, especially when some come from unexpected sources, overwhelms dispassionate analysis. The fact that all of these potential voters say equally kind things to the opposition is not apparent until election day.

Another reason for high morale lies in the nature of a grass roots volunteer organization. Because it is a candidate-centered organization, most of those involved have joined out of loyalty to the candidate or agreement on the issues. The small size and informality of the organization make it a close-knit group. When asked to evaluate his experience as a candidate, Bill replied that while in some ways running was the silliest thing he had ever done, all things considered, it was also one of the best. Despite losing his privacy and taking the risk of public failure, he met many people he liked. He learned a lot about himself and the county he lives in, did some educating of those voters he had direct contact with, and was proud of the campaign he ran. Running even helped him in his job by teaching him more about the practical side of the state legislature. In an age of cynicism about politics it may surprise people that such a positive view of political participation could come from a defeated candidate. But that positive feeling was shared by most of those who worked as volunteers in the campaign.

Scholars have suggested three main incentives for political activity: material, social, and ideological.[5] Given the history of electoral losses by the county Democratic party, material incentives were of little importance to Bill's volunteers. Even for those active within more successful parties, these same studies have indicated that issues are the most important of the three incentives. Furthermore, scholars have found that whatever the initial stimulus, social incentives become more important in sustaining political activity, a finding confirmed here.[6] Social incentives may not have been the primary reason people volunteered to work for Bill, but as the campaign progressed, personal solidarity increased to the point that many of those involved became quite friendly with one another outside the campaign. The organization was small enough so that every one knew one another. Everyone also had significant personal contact with the candidate. These personal relationships reduced the impact of those inevitable disagreements that took place during the campaign.

However, the informality of a volunteer organization also creates serious difficulties. Because Bill had never run for office, he had to build an organization from scratch. A strong party might have been able to help in areas where the candidate's organization was weakest but the Oswego County Democratic Party was rarely in a position to do so. Another problem was that there always seemed to be a crisis or deadline that had to be addressed, resulting in strategies that were too often ad hoc instead of long range. Not being able to have a full-time campaign manager was another disadvantage. Jack had much outside the campaign to worry about. This is a problem endemic to a volunteer campaign—despite a strong commitment to the candidate, volunteers have family and job concerns that often are more important to them. Frequently, volunteers are unable to attend meetings or perform tasks on time due to other commitments.

What about the other factors discussed in the introduction? Let us return to the topics presented there.

Political Parties

One of the major changes in parties discussed earlier was the change from party-centered to candidate-centered campaigns. Clearly, Bill's volunteer organization was dedicated primarily to his election and was dissolved after the election. Nevertheless, the Democratic Party was important both for what it did and what it did not do to help.

In this case, the state Democratic party consisted of three entities: the overall party organization and the campaign committees for the two houses of the state legislature. Because the Democrats were certain to retain control of the Assembly but hoped to wrest control of the Senate from the Republicans, the Senate received far more attention. Clearly, the Democratic Assembly Committee (DAC), as research on similar committees has indicated, targeted its funds primarily to the campaigns that appeared most competitive.[7] When in doubt, they asked candidates to use the poll that they supplied. The difficulty with such an approach was that their standard campaign could not possibly work in a rural district like Oswego, creating a self-fulfilling prophecy of loss. Because Bill Scheuerman could not win, there was no reason to help him. Without the resources from the DAC, Bill's campaign in fact could not succeed, so they were proven correct. Contrast this approach to that taken in a district in Syracuse where Joan Christensen was given a significant amount of money even though her opponent was an incumbent assemblyman. This infusion of funds allowed her to run a series of television advertisements contrasting her positions on abortion and gun control with those of her opponent. As a result, she was able to win an upset victory by a margin of one thousand votes out of nearly forty thousand cast. Had the Democratic party wished to build a statewide organization, providing some money or much needed non-financial assistance—such as sending in someone to produce radio ads for Bill—would have strengthened the party in the long run. The DAC's interest was more immediate: holding the Assembly majority in this election. The rest of the state party had no interest at all in the 117th Assembly District. Thus, it is not surprising that a major study of state and local party organizations ranked the New York State Democratic Party as moderately weak, seventy-seventh of the ninety parties rated. In contrast, the Republican Party was rated as moderately strong at number twelve.[8]

Because the state party showed so little interest, Bill had to rely on the county party. The introduction pointed out the most common activities engaged in by local parties: having a campaign headquarters, distributing literature, arranging fund-raisers, giving money to candidates, organizing phone campaigns, sending mailings, organizing canvassing, buying broadcast time, and using polls. All but the last two were done by a majority of the parties.

The Oswego County Democratic Party was very much like the weaker parties studied by scholars. It had a headquarters with a telephone. This office consisted of a large floorspace with few amenities, just a table and a few chairs. It was poorly kept up (the bathroom needed plumbing repairs). Nevertheless, it did provide some work and storage space. Because the party rarely used it, Lou made it available to candidates. Louise scheduled evening work parties twice a week during most of the election season so that volunteers with free time during those evenings knew that they could drop in for important routine tasks such as stuffing envelopes or filling in election district numbers next to signatures on nominating petitions. The headquarters was also a useful base of

operations for gathering petition signatures, canvassing, or literature distribution. The phone had an answering machine that allowed
voters to contact party officials or candidates without bothering
them at home. However, the lack of staff meant that messages were
not always promptly received or answered. There was also a
rudimentary copying machine that was useful, but not for large
jobs or copies that required a neat appearance. More sophisticated
work required either using scarce campaign funds to hire someone or hoping that a volunteer or interest group would donate
equipment or services.

The party itself had little in the way of money to distribute
to candidates but did provide some seed money that proved particularly important in getting started. Bill was able to use party
money to print cards and literature that he or a volunteer handed
out during early person-to-person campaigning. For the most part,
however, we were on our own when it came to fund-raising. The
one significant party fund-raiser held during the campaign was
Geraldine Ferraro's appearance, which replenished the party's virtually empty coffers but did not trickle down to us.

Most of the other tasks were left to the candidate's own organization. This was true not only for Bill but also for the other candidates on the ticket as well. Although some party committee
members helped, it was primarily as individuals rather than as
party officials. For Bill's phone campaigns the party was unable
even to provide a countywide list of telephone numbers. We eventually found that a few city and town parties, most notably in Fulton, had lists of their own. For the most part, including for the city
of Oswego, it was up to volunteers to look up the numbers of thousands of voters from the names and addresses provided on lists
of those registered. As for mailings, canvassing, and literature distribution, it was again largely up to the candidate to organize and
undertake these tasks. Such modern media campaign tasks as taking polls or buying broadcast time were clearly out of the financial
reach of the local party. Overall, the Oswego County Democratic
Party was well below the norm for providing campaign services
although it did provide some assistance to its candidates.

Did the part-time status of the party chair handicap its efforts?
Given the criticism of Lou by many of those active in the campaign
the obvious answer to this question appears to be yes. But we must
remember the observation quoted in the introduction that the direction of causality is unclear. The party was not weak because it had
a part-time chair; it was a weak party that lacked the resources to

have any type of chair other than a part-time one. Had Lou been a political professional, he might have operated more efficiently. But anyone attending a party committee meeting could see that there were no professionals to choose from. The party had neither money nor expertise in modern campaigning. Its countywide registration disadvantage made prospects for success at best a long shot. In fact, significant offices often went uncontested because no even modestly credible candidate was willing to run. This happened for county clerk and nearly for state senate this time around and happened for assembly twice during the previous three elections. Those critical of Lou's selection of Mary Kay Dowd as a replacement candidate for the Senate failed to offer a viable alternative. It appears to be a more reasonable assertion that the weakness of the party, as symbolized by its part-time chair, hurt Bill Scheuerman's campaign. The Republican Party, after all, dominates county politics with its part-time chair. This supports the hypothesis of Joseph Schlesinger that "in one party dominant constituencies both parties will put forth less effort than in competitive constituencies, but the dominant party will exert itself more than will the minority party."[9]

All parties, whatever their strength, must be involved in selecting candidates to run under their label. Clearly the Eldersveld model of candidate recruitment makes the process seem far more rational than the one that nominated Bill Scheuerman. When Bill decided to run for the assembly there were two other possible candidates, Bill Maroney and Jim McMahon. According to Eldersveld's model the party, after careful screening and consultation, would choose its favored candidate. Although there was considerable discussion by party committee members of the three possibilities, the party itself never really made a choice. Instead it waited for the candidates to sort themselves out, running the risk that all three would drop out in frustration at the delay as one endorsement meeting after another was either postponed or took no action. A second risk was that the party could wind up with the weakest of the three by default. The great advantage of this approach was that it maximized party unity. The party committee never had to rebuff any of the candidates. Thus, it avoided alienating them or their supporters. It also made it likely that the most determined candidate would be chosen. In the end, Bill's nomination was supported by a united party.

Such an approach can only work for a minority party whose nomination is not seen as all that attractive. Because McMahon had spent a substantial amount of his own money in his previous try for the assembly, he was not likely to run without guarantees of significant financial assistance. Nor did Maroney's commitment to running appear very strong. The party's best-known figure, Oswego Mayor John Sullivan, was not interested in entering the race. In contrast, the more desirable Republican nomination had a number of willing aspirants, requiring the party to make a choice. Even after the party leadership endorsed Frances Sullivan, Michael Yerdon wanted the nomination so badly that he challenged that decision in a primary.

Eldersveld's model requires variations by party strength. Perhaps parties could be classified as dominant, two-party competitive, and minority to see if their processes of candidate selection differ. Nevertheless, even though the Oswego County party was not as carefully deliberative as the model suggests, its process was otherwise close to Eldersveld's description. The first stage of discovery, in which candidates the party might support are identified, began at the first endorsement meeting. For the assembly race, these candidates were self-selected. For other races, most of which presented virtually no chance of victory in the general election, the party had to convince people to run if they were to have any candidates at all. For these, once the party found a satisfactory person willing to run, the process should have ended. But, as we saw with Margaret Pavel's senate candidacy, this was not always the case.

Stage two, testing of candidate support, was largely a process of seeing how each individual conducted himself—both in short speeches and conversations with party officials. Because electoral success was so unlikely, getting a satisfactory candidate (one who basically reflected the party's views and would be willing to run an energetic race) was more important than finding the best candidate. Nevertheless, the party did make some attempt to judge the nature of each candidacy—how each would be organized, what kinds of funds would be available, and the issues each would stress. The third stage, sponsorship, turned out to be a formality since the candidates themselves had made the decision. The party played a role by informally indicating to each the extent of his or her support, allowing the candidates to judge their prospects both for the nomination and winning the general election. With no primary, the party did not need to mobilize outside support for its endorsed candidate. Instead, it turned its attention to doing so for the general election.

The final question presented about parties was whether their activities have a significant effect on election results. This race appears to confirm Pomper's view that elections are won and lost by demographic factors and party affiliation rather than party organization. Despite a weak party organization, Bill was able to win more votes than these factors indicated, but not nearly enough to win the election. The Democrats were the weaker of the two parties not so much because they were less well organized, which they were, but because they lacked the voter base of their Republican rivals.

It is, however, worth considering the view of Frendreis, Gibson, and Vertz that where one party is dominant, the other might give less attention to winning the immediate election than to building a presence in the long run.[10] In one sense this was true in Oswego County. The main goal of the Democratic Party, not quite achieved, was to run a full slate of candidates. Still, calling this a long-term strategy makes it sound far more calculated than in fact it was. Even a task as basic as maintaining an up-to-date list of Democratic voters was not attempted. Considering how easy this should be in an age of computer data bases, it is obvious that more sophisticated party-building activities could not be undertaken without help from the state party. However, the state party had virtually no interest in building a stronger party in areas where it was particularly weak. It was unwilling (or perhaps unable due to the scarcity of resources) to commit even small amounts of funds or technical assistance to achieve the goal of long-term party building. All of the state party's efforts seemed focused on short-term goals such as winning current elections and seeking control of the state senate.

Nor did there appear to be any long-term plan by the county party in the selection of candidates. Jerry Herrington was a businessman who had some experience in the County Sheriff's Department. When he volunteered to run, without any real previous party activity, his offer was gladly accepted in the absence of other candidates to oppose the incumbent. The original senate candidate, Margaret Pavel, planned to run a liberal campaign based on her positions in favor of more government programs to assist families and abortion rights. When she withdrew, her replacement was a former local Conservative Party chair with a strong right-to-life stance.

In a district dominated by one party, the main goal of the minority party seems less to select the best candidate than simply to fill its ballot positions. It will first seek to do so with satisfactory candidates—that is, those who generally agree with the party's positions and are willing to campaign energetically. Even this simple goal will often prove too difficult to achieve, forcing the party either to settle for candidates who come up short on one of the two standards or to leave its line vacant for one or more offices. The combination of this concentration on immediate objectives and the limited resources and professionalism of such parties is likely to make long-term strategies an unlikely luxury. This case study tends to support the Pomper view. However, we will later examine other factors that could make minority party electoral success possible even when the demographic and party registration figures are stacked against it.

Campaign Strategy

The introduction described three major tasks facing candidates at the beginning of a campaign: developing an organization, gathering information, and deciding how to present themselves. The beginning of this chapter first discussed the development and maintenance of Bill's organization, then examined the role of the party. Having looked at these two separately, we now must examine the possible strains between the two suggested in the introductory chapter.

Although the party itself encouraged Bill to develop his own organization to perform the tasks that it lacked the resources to provide, that independence did lead to conflict. There was a minor flap at the beginning of the campaign when those gathering signatures for Bill's petitions did not also ask for signatures for petitions for all other Democratic candidates. That would have meant asking each voter to sign ten petitions, including those for state party committee and judicial candidates. The biggest source of tension was the governor's reelection campaign. Although Bill did support Mario Cuomo, the governor's unpopularity in the county, together with Bill's desire to demonstrate his independence from politics as usual, made keeping the two campaigns separate particularly important for him.

In order to have any chance at all, Bill had to win the votes of substantial numbers of independent and Republican voters, something that coupling his campaign too closely to that of the governor would prevent. Appealing to these same voters also meant playing down partisan themes. Thus, some literature made little or no mention of Bill's party affiliation, instead referring to him as the Common Sense candidate, the name of our independent line. These tensions came to a head during our literature drop the Saturday before the election. At the last minute, the party asked Bill to include Cuomo literature along with his own. Not wishing to do so, Bill offered to have a group of volunteers distribute that literature the following Monday, an offer that so aggravated the party that it apparently led to some of the shouting referred to in my journal entry for November 3.

The modern campaign relies on polling as a primary tool of intelligence gathering but, as suggested in the introduction, lack of funds prevented Bill from doing so. The DAC had asked him to take a poll in order to allow them to judge whether he had enough of a chance of victory for them to contribute funds. Because the prepackaged questions on the poll bore little relation to Bill's strategy, the results would not have supplied him with much useful data. In addition, there would have been a number of potential sources of error due to the use of volunteers, timing, and the nature of the sample.

We had hoped to design our own poll instead. We went so far as to draw up a questionnaire and discuss how to take the survey. Unfortunately, there were so many other high-priority tasks to perform with our limited resources that the poll was postponed several times. By then our strategy was so well set that we decided taking a poll would be a poor allocation of those resources. In retrospect, the considerable time and energy devoted to the independent petitions could have been better used to take a benchmark poll before the Republican primary and a follow-up during the second half of October to help assess our progress. The independent line turned out to be of little use, garnering a mere 493 votes. Since many of these would probably have voted for Bill even without the second line, the considerable effort we spent getting it proved largely wasted. Had an early poll been taken instead, the results might have led us to target our advertising better and clarify our message. It would also have been a check on the optimism we were beginning to feel.

Despite some efforts to gather information from a canvass, the district proved so large and spread out that going door to door to speak to large numbers of voters was out of the question. In a number of towns, especially in the northern part of the county, we either relied on others, such as the Yerdons, to turn out favorable voters, or we simply wrote the towns off (with perhaps an appearance or two by Bill to show the flag and pick up a few votes) in order to concentrate on more supportive areas with larger populations. When we did knock on doors, it was primarily to drop off literature. We spoke briefly if someone was home, but our goal was to cover as many households as possible. Most canvassing was by telephone, an operation that got going fairly late in the campaign, largely due to the need to develop our own list of phone numbers. The prime goal of the telephone canvass was to identify potentially supportive voters who could be called again on Election Day to remind them to vote. The inability to call all voters limited us to those most likely to support Bill: (1) registered Democrats; (2) members of unions that had endorsed him; and (3) independents, especially those who had signed Bill's petitions. Because the telephone canvass was designed for these other tasks, it could not be of much use as a systematic intelligence-gathering tool.

As a result, Bill was forced, as Hershey suggested, to look to political activists, many of whom were among his strongest supporters. Even the large number of voters he spoke to were either already supporting him (otherwise they would have been at home or at a Fran Sullivan appearance) or simply too polite to tell a candidate they were going to vote for his opponent. The same was true of our telephone canvass. Clearly this was, as has already been pointed out, one reason for our ungrounded optimism. On some issues, such as the death penalty or approval of Governor Cuomo, traditional sources of information proved quite accurate. Whether they prevented us from learning that one of Bill's issues could have been further developed into a successful appeal is something we will never know. What is clear is that as constituencies grow in population, traditional forms of learning about the wishes of voters are largely inadequate. Whatever their limitations, polls have become a necessity for candidates running for legislatures, except in those states whose districts remain fairly small.

Hershey's third task was deciding how to present the candidate. The introduction discussed Joslyn's four types of appeals: partisan, personal characteristics of the candidates, demographic groups, and issues. In the last category, he suggested three different issue appeals: issue salience; vague, ambiguous, or symbolic appeals; and specific policy positions. His research found relatively few partisan and specific issue appeals. Instead, candidates preferred to use issues to illustrate their personal characteristics and to appeal to groups.

The large party registration disadvantage made partisan appeals a hopeless tactic. Bill sought to make a virtue out of necessity by stressing his own independence. Much of his advertising and campaign material failed to mention his party. He often pointed out that because the state party was giving him no funds, he would not be indebted to them if elected. But this did not mean that there were no party appeals. As part of his theme of aggressive representation, he pointed out that any Republican would be part of the assembly minority and therefore frozen out of major decisions. When asked whether there was a contradiction between being so independent and being part of the decision-making majority, he was able to explain how he would be able to balance the two. Overall, however, it was the theme of independence that took precedence over partisan appeals.

In the primary campaign, all of Sullivan's advertising emphasized that she was the officially endorsed Republican candidate. For the general election she continued some partisan appeals, either positively by stressing the virtues of the Republican Party such as opposition to tax increases or negatively by attacking the Democratic Party as dominated by New York City and therefore likely to send money from central New York downstate.

Personal characteristics were an important part of Bill's appeal. The large number of appearances he made (far more than his opponent) was an attempt to show as many people as possible his intelligence and energy. He hoped to showcase the contrast between himself and his opponent by scheduling as many joint appearances as possible, a strategy that the Sullivan campaign was able to resist. Much of his advertising and literature stressed such personal attributes as his successful experience as Minetto Town Supervisor, working his way through college and graduate school while raising a family, and his experience as an educator and union leader.

Sullivan's ads also emphasized the personal. This was especially true of her late negative advertising that pointed to Bill's New York City origins as a reason to suspect that he would be a prisoner of the downstate Democrats in the legislature.

Bill's appeals sought to picture him as the advocate of average people, especially workers and small farmers. He stressed his own background and the endorsements by unions for the former. Members of unions that had endorsed him were sent a packet pointing this out, then called to remind them to vote. A significant amount of his advertising sought to show how important farm issues were for him. Pictures of him appearing with prominent farm leaders and politicians who had demonstrated concern for agriculture were included in several newspaper advertisements and press releases. Bill also hoped to appeal to consumers through his support of item pricing.

As for issues, Bill's appeals tended to focus on issue salience rather than specific proposals. However, there were a few particulars such as support for item pricing, several pieces of farm legislation, and the legislative salary freeze. Capital punishment was discussed only when someone asked. Abortion was never a subject of any advertisements. During the debate, a number of issues including abortion (specifically proposals requiring parental notification for minors), incineration, the Route 481 bypass of Fulton, and the budget were discussed but, given the nature of the post-debate media coverage, that discussion turned out to have virtually no importance. Because it became apparent early in the campaign that specific issue appeals would receive little media attention, the candidates had no incentive to engage in them. Sullivan's advertising had even less specific issue content than Bill's. It stressed her opposition to increasing taxes and suggested that cutting spending was a better approach but offered few specifics about what programs she would cut. While Bill argued that both parties shared some blame for the state's budget problems due to the divided control of the legislature, she aimed her fire at the Democrats because of their control of both the assembly and the governorship.

The most difficult issue to handle was capital punishment. Bill had great reservations about it but it was clear that the voters were overwhelmingly in favor. A few months after the election, he told me of his belief that the death penalty was a "bogus" issue because such a "quick fix" would do little to reduce crime. He eventually decided that a trade-off had to be made. His personal feelings became less important than keeping open the prospect of discussing other issues. As a candidate he needed credibility. He expected only to be able to educate voters incrementally and in the long run. Since even with his support of capital punishment, he never was able to discuss other aspects of the crime issue he was uncertain whether he would handle it the same way if he had a second chance.[11]

Overall, Joslyn's observations were confirmed by the appeals of the candidates in this assembly district. The one difference was that due to their large registration advantage, the Republican Party used partisan themes more than the candidates Joslyn studied.

Campaign Spending

Bill's campaign was more candidate- than party-centered; but otherwise the modern style of campaign seems barely to have touched this assembly district. Clearly Bill's effort was far more in line with old-fashioned politics. Its prime strategy was to expose as many people as possible to the candidate, then supplement that by direct mail. Nevertheless, even such a traditional campaign had elements of the more modern style. Bill did run a series of radio advertisements even if they were not professionally produced. He depended very much on the media covering some of his appearances and discussing the issues he raised to reach those voters who were not at events he attended.

Although the Sullivan campaign was more professionally handled—hiring a public relations firm that produced advertising and spending considerably more money—it too fit more closely to the old style. Neither candidate advertised on television. In the primary, Sullivan remained in the background, depending upon the party endorsement pulling enough voters in a low turnout to win the nomination. During the general election she minimized not only debates but also the kind of public appearances that would generate media coverage, apparently believing that such appearances would also generate stories about her opponent. Thus, her campaign was relatively low key until the charges at the end of the debate and her negative radio ads shortly before the election. She hoped to win primarily on the basis of the Republican Party's overwhelming registration advantage.

Overall, very little of the modern campaign has filtered down to Oswego County as evidenced by the total spending of both candidates of about $75,000. Our discussion of the mass media will return to this topic.

Interest Groups

During this campaign, interest groups provided significant support to Bill's candidacy that the party was unable to. The most obvious was money but in-kind contributions were equally important. Most notable were the membership lists and phone banks provided by the unions. In the absence of a party mailing and telephone list these were crucial for targeting and mobilizing voters. In this case, groups stepped in to fill a vacuum left by a relatively weak party. Had these groups not existed, Bill's candidacy would have been weaker but the party would not have been stronger. Thus, it can be fairly stated that some candidates in a largely one-party area may be willing to run against the dominant party because they know that interest group support is available. This can strengthen two-party competition depending upon the particular interests and strengths of those groups. Interestingly enough, the kind of single-issue group so decried by some critics of contemporary American politics was not much in evidence in this campaign.[12]

Unfortunately for Bill, interest group assistance fell far short of what was needed to make up for party weakness. As discussed in the introduction, most PAC money is contributed to incumbents. Even when there is an open seat, a candidate of a minority party needs to show a significant likelihood of success in order to get contributions. As with the state party, interest groups placed Bill in the untenable position of having to prove his viability in order to get the money required to make him viable.

Unlike the more modern campaign, the type we conducted relies far more on personal connections to gain interest group support. Bill was able to convince NYSUT, the statewide teachers union, to endorse him, resulting in both monetary and in-kind contributions, because he was an officer of one of its locals. Thus, NYSUT's policy of rarely endorsing nonincumbents was bypassed because of Bill's proven record and his personal acquaintance with many of its officers. Similarly, Bill was backed by the prison guards' union because he had worked with them in the past. Bill's connection to Dave Turner and the work of both with local labor groups helped bring in some other union endorsements.

Of course, there was also a downside to the personal factor. Some groups that might have endorsed Bill because of agreement on the issues stayed silent because they did not know him. In other cases, personal connections of the opposition enabled them to gain support from groups that to us seemed far closer to Bill on the issues. One example was the endorsement of the local Civil Service Employees Association. Fran Sullivan did not even answer their questionnaire, yet she received their endorsement. Another group endorsed her even before Bill had decided to run, making it clear that they had not compared the two.

Media Coverage

To most of the local media the assembly election was not a particularly important story. Even during late September or October there were weeks during which perhaps a single story appeared in the main daily, the *Oswego Palladium-Times*. Area radio stations generally limited themselves to a total of five minutes at a time for all local news, making thorough coverage an impossibility. When they did cover the campaign, it was generally tied to a specific event with a ten-second sound bite from one or both candidates.

Thus, the biggest problem for the candidates was not one of getting thorough coverage of issues but getting any coverage at all. The numerous events Bill went to were rarely considered newsworthy by the media. His regular news releases received little coverage. No one expected them to be published verbatim but surely those based on issues could have led reporters to question the candidates on those topics. What coverage there was tended to focus on drama and conflict of a personal nature. This supports the critics quoted in the introduction. The stories about the debate and its follow-up are the best examples, although hardly the only ones. There was one profile of the two candidates in the Oswego County section of the *Syracuse Post Standard* that briefly summarized their positions on several important issues. *Eye on City Hall* ran long interviews with all three candidates (Yerdon included) during September and printed one of Bill's and one of Fran's press releases each week. The *Oswego Valley News* usually ran a story on the campaign but it is not a daily and few of the stories said much about issues. Bill ran several of his press releases as ads in the weeklies. Even had a conscientious voter read every newspaper in the county, he or she would have had a difficult time learning the positions of the candidates on the major issues. More likely, someone would rely on a single paper or radio station.

For television the race did not exist. There were no stories about it on any newscasts of the three network affiliates in Syracuse. The closest was during Geraldine Ferraro's appearance in Oswego when a careful viewer could see Bill in the background. Yet these same stations frequently covered news of Oswego County, especially crimes, accidents, or human interest items. Occasionally they even sent the anchors to a site in Oswego County to originate a live broadcast. Some of the towns in southern Oswego County are in fact, as close to Syracuse as to the city of Oswego and far closer than to Redfield or Richland in the north. Virtually all of the homes from the city of Oswego south as well as many to the north are primarily served by Syracuse television. However, those stations gave the assembly election absolutely no coverage.

Did this matter in the end? For Bill to win he would have had to find an issue that had resonance with voters and communicate to them the differences on that issue between himself and his opponent. Such communication could only occur by means of the mass media. However, Bill never was able to get hold of a galvanizing issue. Despite some success in communicating Bill's qualifications, his campaign had little luck in spreading an issue-oriented message. Bill's theme was a populist one, aiming at increasing democracy and voter involvement. Despite the effectiveness of this in person, it did not appeal to the media. The salary freeze, jobs, proposals to improve the budget process, consumer issues, attacks on the unfairness of the tax system, and environmental issues never caught on. He tried to discuss the issue of safety of nuclear power but it too received little press. When he attacked the Department of Environmental Conservation for favoring big polluters while prosecuting small ones the issue proved too complex for significant coverage. The abortion issue fizzled when Fran Sullivan changed her position, and despite Bill's efforts during the debate and other appearances to point that out, the media never pursued the matter. Without either a strong party organization or the funds for a modern media-oriented campaign, the only way to communicate issues was through free media. But local reporters had little interest in policy issues. Instead, there was charge and reply, allowing Sullivan to set the agenda with her statement at the end of the debate. She was able to get by with few specifics, coasting in on the Republican registration edge and the fear of downstate liberal Democrats.

An issue-based campaign could only have succeeded for Bill if the media had given policy issues enough coverage to make voters aware of the differences between candidates. We have already seen that this was not the case. The lack of issues coverage in the media meant that the onus of communicating his message fell on Bill. The district, however, was too large to communicate a message purely through personal appearances. Only through a modern media campaign could Bill have succeeded.

The previously mentioned campaign of Joan Christensen offers a contrast. In essence, through her advertising, Christensen set the campaign agenda. For Bill this was impossible, primarily due to lack of funds. Because Oswego has no television stations of its own (unlike Christensen's Syracuse district) he would have had to advertise on Syracuse television, most of whose viewers are not in Oswego County. Even Sullivan, with considerably more resources than Bill, chose not to do this. Clearly, media markets shape the nature of campaigns. A future study might attempt to relate media markets to campaign expenditures.

Evaluating the Campaign

From the point of view of the voter, the answer to Eldersveld's question of how well the campaign contributed to meaningful participation and deliberation is: not well at all. Those voters who were able to see the candidates either at the debate or other personal appearances were often able to learn their positions on policy issues and judge their qualifications. However, most citizens lacked the information necessary for an informed evaluation of the candidates. Nor was there much debate between the candidates, in the media, or among the electorate about what direction New York State should go, what Oswego County needed, or what the public really wanted from its representatives. The major success of the campaign was that it energized a significant number of people, albeit a small fraction of the electorate, to get involved in or increase their involvement in politics. These volunteers, win or lose, learned a lot about the political system, got a chance to express their views, and are likely to continue their involvement. For them, there was a spirited contest between the two candidates but otherwise there was little that touched the lives of most residents of the county. It will be left to the judgment of each reader to allocate responsibility.

We found that the 117th Assembly District election was for the most part conducted in traditional fashion yet even such a contest had elements of the modern media campaign. Radio advertising was important to both candidates. Sullivan hired a public relations firm to produce her commercials and help plan strategy. Had television been more accessible or less expensive, it would have been used. Subsequent to the campaign, area cable systems began selling advertising, making it likely that future candidates will be able to make more use of television. Both candidates sought favorable news coverage. It is probable that future assembly campaigns will make at least limited use of polls. Even the relatively weak county Democratic Party is likely to begin to generate computerized lists of voters.

Does this mean that within a short period of time the traditional campaign will be largely a relic? With the high cost of the media campaign, the limited access to television in non-media market districts like Oswego County, and the relative weakness of the party organizations involved, that appears unlikely. More probable is the development of a hybrid campaign, bringing in some modern techniques while retaining much of the traditional structure and tactics. On the local level, especially in non-urban districts, such campaigns are likely to be common and therefore deserving of more study.

Particularly important are the roles of the party and the media. Where candidates can run a modern campaign, they are able to overcome news inattention by spending large sums of money on advertising.[13] In the hybrid campaigns, however, those running get the worst of both worlds. Traditional person-to-person and party organizational methods of getting the message directly to voters are either impractical in districts of increasing size or impossible given the changing nature of the party. If the media give lower-level campaigns little coverage while devoting nearly all of that coverage to personalities and drama, voters will lack the information about candidate qualifications and issues necessary to cast an intelligent vote. Unable to afford the media blitz necessary to overcome this, those running for office will find the exercise a frustrating experience. In one-party dominant areas, these factors may also make it more difficult for the minority party to become more competitive without outside help from interest groups or the state or national party. There are more such areas than one might think even in competitive two-party states. As Joseph Aistrup has written, New York "is one of the better examples of how the state-level party competitive average masks the county-level nature of party competition. . . . Not many of New York's counties are two-party competitive. The GOP controls upstate New York and Long Island, while only the New York City area is a Democratic stronghold." He found similar patterns in a number of other states.[14] Thus, if state parties target only the closer races, they will attract most of the money and attention, leaving the others largely uncontested.[15]

With so much attention being paid to declining voter participation,[16] such a trend could only make the situation worse. Reforms should have two major goals: ensuring adequate party competition to allow the voters a meaningful choice in virtually all elections, and providing those voters with enough information about issues and candidate qualifications to allow them to make that choice rationally. There are many possibilities.[17] One is public financing of campaigns. This would allow enough money for at least two candidates in each contest to have adequately funded campaigns. A second is to require television and radio stations to give a certain amount of time to each candidate. This could be made a requirement of federal licensing. Candidates would be given a microphone and asked to explain in ten or fifteen minutes why they should be elected. The two ideas could be combined by requiring candidates who accept public funding to participate in a certain number of debates.

Nor should change be confined to reforming the law. In exchange for the rights granted them under the First Amendment, the media have a responsibility to inform the public. All election contests should be given serious consideration and that consideration should include discussion of the qualifications of the candidates and the major issues dividing them. It is clear that the public is dissatisfied with the political process. As W. Lance Bennett has written, "If journalists shifted their priorities and held candidates accountable for ideas instead of idiosyncrasies, they just might find a resurgence of support."[18]

The main advantage of the old-fashioned grass-roots campaign was that it allowed direct participation by the public. It required many volunteers to get out the candidate's message. The parties provided an institution for maintaining such activity on a regular basis. At the same time, much of the public had direct contact with either candidates or their representatives. The fact that campaigns like the one examined in this book still exist allows some continuation of that form of empowerment, but the modern campaign is increasing the distance between politicians and the public. We need to find a way to narrow that gap.

Notes

1. Election results were obtained from the Oswego County Board of Elections.

2. My many informal conversations with Bill about the campaign were supplemented by a more formal interview on May 22, 1991.

3. Spending totals are from the candidate reports filed January 1991 with the New York State Board of Elections.

4. Theodore H. White, *The Making of the President, 1972* (New York: Bantam Books, 1973), pp. 453–454.

5. Paul Allan Beck and Frank J. Sorauf, *Party Politics in America*, 7th ed. (New York: HarperCollins, 1992), pp. 115–125. Beck and Sorauf summarize most of the major studies on this subject.

6. M. Margaret Conway, "Political Parties and Political Mobilization," *The American Review of Politics* 14 (Winter 1993), pp. 549–563.

7. Two examples are Anthony Gierzynski, *Legislative Party Campaign Committees in the American States* (Lexington, Ky.: University Press of Kentucky, 1992) and Mildred A. Schwartz, "Electoral Success Versus Party Maintenance: National, State, and Local Party Contributions to Illinois Legislative Races," *Publius: The Journal of Federalism* 24 (Winter 1994), pp. 79–92.

8. Cornelius Cotter, James Gibson, John Bibby, and Robert Huckshorn, *Party Organizations in American Politics* (New York: Praeger, 1984), pp. 28–29.

9. Joseph A. Schlesinger, "The New American Political Party," *The American Political Science Review* 79 (Dec. 1985), p. 1154.

10. John P. Frendreis, James L. Gibson, and Laura L. Vertz, "The Electoral Relevance of Local Party Organizations," *American Political Science Review* 84 (March 1990), pp. 225–235.

11. Interview, 1991.

12. For a discussion of campaigns in which single issue groups played an important role, see Marjorie Randon Hershey and Darrell M. West, "Single-Issue Politics: Prolife Groups and the 1980 Senate Campaign," in Allan J. Cigler and Burdett A. Loomis (eds.), *Interest Group Politics* (Washington, D.C.: CQ Press, 1983), pp. 31–59.

13. Some studies have found that even in presidential elections, commercials may have more issue content than television news. For example, see Thomas E. Patterson and Robert D. McClure, *The Unseeing Eye: The Myth of Television Power in National Elections* (New York: G.P. Putnam's Sons, 1976). A more recent view, including both national and state elections, is Darrell M. West, *Air Wars: Television Advertising in Election Campaigns, 1952–1992* (Washington, D.C.: Congressional Quarterly, 1993).

14. Joseph A. Aistrup, "State Legislative Party Competition: A County-Level Measure," *Political Research Quarterly* 46 (June 1993), p. 442.

15. Gierzynski, 1992, p. 120.

16. For example, see Walter Dean Burnham, *The Current Crisis in American Politics* (New York: Oxford University Press, 1982) and Michael M. Gant and Norman R. Luttbeg, *American Electoral Behavior: 1952–1988* (Itasca, Ill.: F.E. Peacock, 1991), chapters 3 and 4.

17. For example, see Mark Green, "Take the Money and Reform," in Stephen J. Wayne and Clyde Wilcox, *The Quest for National Office* (New York: St. Martin's Press, 1992), pp. 322–327; and W. Lance Bennett, *The Governing Crisis* (New York: St. Martin's Press, 1992), chapter 8.

18. Bennett, 1992, p. 214.